THE ROI OF MEMBERSHIP

TODAY'S MISSING LINK FOR EXPLOSIVE GROWTH

Other books by Ed Rigsbee

The Art of Partnering

Developing Strategic Alliances

Partner*Shift*

Brian Gets to Play

Kids, Parents & Soccer

The ROI Of Membership

Today's Missing Link for Explosive Growth

Ed Rigsbee, CAE

The ROI of Membership

Today's Missing Link for Explosive Growth

Published by Ryjon Publishing, Thousand Oaks, CA 91360
Orders: www.rigsbee.com

Unattributed quotations are by Ed Rigsbee.

Edition ISBN; Softcover 978-0-9785434-0-2
First Edition, First Printing 2014

Cover design by Ryan Rigsbee

Printed in the United States of America by
McNaughton & Gunn, Inc.
Saline, Michigan 48176

Table of Contents

Acknowledgements ix
Foreward xiii
Preface xv

How this Member ROI Measuring Came About xix

Chapter 1: Why Organizations Should Know Their Real-Dollar ROI of Membership 1

Priceless is Not a Member Recruitment Strategy 3
You Say Employers Aren't Paying Anymore? 4
The Right Tools 5
State the ROI 6
Associations Morphing Into Communities of Reciprocity 7
Associations Competing with Google 8
Know the Players—Two Important Emotional Categories of Association Members 9
ROI Numbers Necessary for All Recruitment Campaigns 10
Chapter 1 Executive Action Steps: 12

Chapter 2: Member-Only Reigns Supreme 13

Don't Get Lost in the Weeds 14
The Wrong Perspective 17
Land Mine in the Making 18
Industry Stakeholder Benefit 21
Member-Only Benefit 21
Is Your Website Recruiting? 22
Getting Them to Join and Stay 23
Chapter 2 Executive Action Steps: 25

Chapter 3: Research Methods That Work 27

Quantitative Research 27
Qualitative Research 29

There's Room for Both 31

Active Qualitative Research Focus Group Methodology 32
Rejected Research 34
Chapter 3 Executive Action Steps: 35

Chapter 4: The Rigsbee Member ROI Valuation Process™ 37

Benefit of Member-Determined Numbers 37
Valuing Different Features 40
Selling the Idea to Board and Staff 40
Get the Correct Facilitator 41
Get a Pro 41
Selecting Membership Samples 43
Vendor Value 44
Generational Value 46
Gathering Sample Groups 47
Measure Just Member-Only Features 48

Conducting Your Qualitative Research 49

Facilitator Guidelines for Active Focus Group Method: 49
Qualitative Focus Group Process Steps 50
How it Might Look 55
Group Dynamics 57
Disruptive Personalities 57

Interview Method 60

What's Next After the Facilitation? 62
Chapter 4 Executive Action Step: 65

Chapter 5: Know What Each Feature of Membership is Worth 67

Looking for Additional ROI in All the Right Places 68
Unintended ROI Killer 71
Communities of Reciprocity—an Important Feature of Membership 72
Member Created and Administered Communities 74
Organization-Generated Communities 75
Organization-Assisted Communities 77

Put a Price on Everything 78
What Else Do You Have to Sell? 79
Specific Features of Membership 81
Professional Development ROI Numbers 83
Business Solution ROI Numbers 84
Knowledge Management ROI Numbers 85
Networking ROI Numbers 86
What to Keep & What to Dump 86
How to Conduct the Features of Membership Value Discovery Exercise 88
Chapter 5 Executive Action Steps 93

Chapter 6: Start Selling Value, Not Guilt 95

Feature versus Benefit 96

Feature of Membership Benefit Statements 97

Professional Development Benefit Copy 98
Business Solution Benefit Copy 100
Knowledge Management Benefit Copy 103
Networking Benefit Copy 105

Buying Motives 106

Profit and Gain 107
Fear of Loss 107
Avoidance of Pain 108
Comfort and Pleasure 108
Love and Affection 109
Pride and Prestige 110
Sell to the Primary 111
Value Triangle 112
Chapter 6 Executive Action Steps 115

Chapter 7: Membership is Everybody's Business 117

Three Recruitment Methods 117
Which Model is Right for You? 118
Method Challenges 119
Embarrassingly Enough... 121

Your Four-Step Organic Grassroots Member Recruitment Campaign 122

Board-Driven Acceleration 129

The Art and Science of Member Evangelism 131

The Evangelistic Member Lifecycle Model 131
Shift Your Culture to Member Recruitment Evangelism 133
Staff Culture 134
Member Culture 136
Evangelism—What's In It for the Baby Boomers? 136
Evangelism—What's In It for the Other Generations? 137
All Association Members Must Become Evangelists 137
Suppliers are Members Too 140
What about Staff? 140
Staff Enablers 141
Volunteer versus Staff-Driven Evangelism 141
Staff-Driven Recruitment Effort: 142
Volunteer-Driven Recruitment Effort 143
The Partnership Model 145
Build Your Brand 146
Show Evangelists the Money 148
Evangelists & Incentives 149
Evangelists' Role in New Member Assimilation 150
Changing Member Recruiters' Motivation 151
Converting the Contrarian Member to Evangelism 151
Senior Members & Sacred Cows 154
How do you help an ironclad mind to open up? Perhaps oil and leverage will do the trick? 156
Senior Concerns & Sacred Cow Killing 156
Chapter 7 Executive Action Steps: 160

Prologue 161
Member ROI Summit™ 163
Glossary of Terms 165
About the Author 167

Acknowledgements

Clearly, it takes more than one person to develop and write a comprehensive "how to" book like the one you hold in your hands. I'd like to offer my sincerest thanks and gratitude to the following persons for providing me with feedback, recommendations, editing, new ideas, and alternative perspectives throughout the various drafts of this book:

Sam Albrecht, CAE, Tony Alessandra, Ph.D., Suze Baez, Ph.D., Sophie Bart, Shari Bates, CAE, Celia Trigo Besore, MBA, CAE, Lina Khouri Bush, Mark Buzan, APR/CAE, Andrew Calhoun CAE, William Carbone, Anne Carman, Hannes Combest, Myra Corrello, Ph.D., Michelle Del Marmol, Eric Duchinsky, CAE, Joanne Gerow, Kimberly Gill, Mark Golden, FASAE, CAE, Kay Marsh Green, Phyllis Grummon, Ph.D., Eve Humphreys, MBA, CAE, Sharon Hunt, CAE, Jack Hutson, CAE, SJ Kalian, CAE, Mary Kelly, PhD, Elizabeth Ward Langston, CAE, Kyle Lanning, JD, Adele Lash, Louise Lobinske, Peter Johnson, Ph.D., Janine McBee, CUDE, CMM, Matt Merrigan, Trevor Mitchell, CAE, Terry Monroe, CAE, Charles Morris, Greg Morrison, CAE, Laurel Nelson-Rowe, CQIA, Larry Ohlhauser, MD, Tom Oser, Ph.D., Terry Paulson, Ph.D., Rob Pennington. Ph.D., Jim Phelps, Joachim de Posada, Ph.D., Marilen Reimer, CAE, Ryan Rigsbee, Wendy Roan, Morgan Robinson, Cheryl Ronk, FASAE, CAE, CMP, Bill Schankel, CAE, Lynn Sedlak, CAE, MBA, Cynthia Simpson, M.Ed, CGMP, CAE, Shelley Sykes, Ph.D., Leslie Shivers, CAE, Cynthia Simpson, M.Ed, CGMP, CAE, Andy Steggles, Ysabel Suarez, Marilyn Tam, Ph.D., Stacy Tetschner, FASAE, CAE, Jim Thompson, IOM, CAE, Robert Thomson, CAE, Leonard Toenjes, CAE, Raymond Towle, IOM, CAE, Lindsey Turnau, Jennifer Van Elzen, Bruce Weinstein, Ph.D., Alan Weiss, Ph.D., Lelan Woodmansee, CAE, Harold Wong, Ph.D.

I'd also like to thank my wife of 40 years, Regina Rigsbee. In addition to tolerating my ups and downs throughout the writing and production of this book—she also "endlessly" read chapters for ease of understanding, flow, and mistakes.

A special thank you to my eldest son, Ryan Rigsbee, for his Gen Y perspective, crunching the survey numbers, help with graphs, book consistency, and also the book cover design. It's got to be a great day in anybody's book when one gets to work with their adult child on any project.

After two years of concept and writing turmoil—assembling chapters and then tearing them apart, Steve Gordon, my close friend of over four decades, allowed me the use of his home in Naples, Florida for the month of February 2013. With only a card table as a deck, that was the escape I needed to finally formulate and produce the first draft of this iteration, which eventually became this book. Without that month-long get-away, this book would have continued to languish.

Thanks to the individuals in my professional speaker mastermind group, the Gold Coast Institute, for tolerating over a year of questions—and for strategic and tactical support in making this book what it is today: Carlos Conejo, CSSBB, W Mitchell, CSP, CPAE, Terry Paulson, Ph.D., CSP, CPAE, Dan Poynter, CSP, Marilyn Tam, Ph.D., Sandra Dee Robinson, Robert Tucker, Bill Wagner, CSP, and Jim Zinger, CSP. Just a word on the benefit of mastermind groups, we have been meeting approximately monthly since the winter of 1988-1989. Many have come and gone, however three of the original four, (Terry Paulson, Robert Tucker and me) are still active. Every member of this group, past and present, have been and are, exceedingly precious to me.

I also believe it's important to mention the two executive directors that took an early chance on engaging me to conduct my full-day member recruitment workshop, *"Want More Members—Give 'em More ROI."* The workshop is truly the genesis of this book and predecessor to the Member ROI Summit™. Thanks to Patricia Koziol, Executive Director at the Mid-Atlantic Society of Association executives and Joan "JT" Tezak, CAE, CMP, Executive Director at the Colorado Society of Association Executives.

To close the acknowledgements, it was Cynthia D'Amour, in a little Honolulu restaurant that set me on a path to increase my personal capacity beyond author, consultant, and professional speaker to include professional association executive. Then it was Greg Melia, CAE that convinced me to earn my Certified Association Executive (CAE) credential and suggested that I take the Michigan Society of Association Executives' (MSAE) online prep-course. Through this course, Cheryl Ronk, FASAE, CAE, CMP, and Sue Radwan, MEd., ARM, CAE, SMP do a magnificent job in helping association executives prepare for the CAE exam. I would absolutely be remiss if I didn't thank them all for their insight, knowledge, and especially in my case—patience. Cheryl's famous line was, *"Ed, do you want to be right or do you want to pass?"* I do not believe I would have passed the CAE exam without taking the MSAE course. The path to earning my CAE has had a strong influence on my perspective and knowledge, which is clearly manifested in the final version of this book.

Foreward

The ROI of Membership is edgy. It's one of those infrequent gems that challenges common practice, debunks bad advice about what to do instead, and provides a practical roadmap of how to do it right.

The association eco-system tends to be perpetually awash with noise about the future of membership as an organizational model. Since the advent of the internet, false prophets have predicted the end of membership as a business model. Alternatively, well intentioned supporters have defended the business model by waving the flags of volunteerism, community and common good. Ed Rigsbee settles the dispute by providing a proven method to make the business case for membership as a business model.

The ROI of Membership recognizes that perceived value is what sustains engagement and the demonstration of tangible value is what earns the perception. Until this book, the process of discovering, identifying, quantifying, and communicating the tangible value of membership has eluded too many worthy organizations.

Ed Rigsbee has provided his colleagues with the final elusive piece for today's member recruitment puzzle. Based on insight drawn from years of experience as a business and nonprofit executive and advisor, he has laid out a step-by-step process to determine and convey value to current and prospective members in terms that will have meaning to them.

The ROI of Membership is a practical, no-nonsense handbook for how membership driven organizations can meaningfully and honestly articulate their value proposition. It provides a methodology, along with explanation, about why and how you go through the ROI process and then use your findings to grow and retain members

This book is a truly groundbreaking work. It is different from any other "member recruitment" book available today. It offers both strategy and tactics for proving ***The***

ROI of Membership, in real dollar numbers. It enables associations to demonstrate the business mindset that members want to see accompany dedication to their cause. And, it provides a means for association executives to embed sustained commitment to a relevant, compelling, and quantified value proposition into the association's culture.

Glenn Tecker
Chairman and Co-CEO Tecker International LLC
Primary co-author of three bestselling books:
The Will To Govern Well: *Knowledge, Trust and Nimbleness*
Building a Knowledge-Based Culture: *Using 21st Century Work and Decision-Making Systems in Associations*
Successful Association Leadership: *Dimensions of 21st Century Competency for the CEO*

Preface

Thank you for **investing in this book**, I can assure you an excellent return. Just think, if you were only to recruit one new member based on what you learned in this book—and retained that member for ten years—you would have received a very reasonable return on your investment (ROI). However, that is not enough—not by a long-shot. If you read this book in its entirety and actually follow the steps, your organization should enjoy a bare minimum 5-10% INCREASE in new memberships and a similar percentage in increased retention. Study the book and implement the ideas, your organization should expect explosive growth. How much additional revenue per year would that equal for the small investment you have made in this book?

The various drafts of this book have passed through the hands of about 200 association executives and content experts. Many asked **for whom was this book written**. Before that question is answered, you must first know this book was written as a comprehensive how-to guide offering both strategy and tactics for a unique approach to member recruitment and retention. With that in mind, the answer to that question is everyone from the chief staff executive (CSE) to the newest member services intern. This book was also written with volunteer leaders in mind. I firmly believe that every person that sits on your board of directors should have their own copy, along with "membership" and "member services" committee chairs. The title of the last chapter says it all: "*Membership is Everybody's Business.*"

In the text of this book I frequently mention "executives" as a catch-all term for all staff members in a decision-making capacity. If you are a director of membership, I didn't forget about you.

My first book, *The Art of Partnering*, was published 20 years ago in 1994. During those years of consulting, presenting keynotes, concurrent sessions, and multi-day workshops for both associations and corporations, I clearly learned that "partnering" starts in the executive suite. Similarly, I have come to absolutely believe that **truly effective member recruitment must emanate from the CSE**. Not that this person must have a daily hands-on role but this person must be the cheer leader and driver of the effort—holding steadfast to the idea of explosive member growth and market expansion. Everyone watches what this person does much more than they listen to what he/she says. Truly, "*Membership is Everybody's Business.*"

One executive that reviewed the second draft of this book stated the following, *"Given that I know you, and your personality, I was comfortable with some of the* ***more brash tone*** *or text. Yet, others may not 'get it' or accept it. That, too, may be something that you set up in an introduction or foreward."* So let me set this up now, I am an unapologetic contrarian—plain and simple.

Let me explain how this serves you...I see different patterns and holes in the people, organizations, products, and services that I study. For example, I started a 501(c)(3) resulting from a hole in services I discovered at a particular organization for which I was at the time, and still am today, a member. The non-profit continues today, serving a particular constituency at that association. The non-profit has also successfully created events and services that the association has taken over. **Everybody wins when everybody is served.** It is that approach that I have brought to the ideas in this book—spotting holes—to help you better serve your members, deliver more ROI, and attract the uninitiated. This book is designed to challenge—even the very best.

Some feedback I also received was that the book really starts at Chapter 4. While there may be some truth to that, the earlier chapters are necessary to correctly build the foundation upon which the "meat" of the book rests. If you are already sold on the value and validity of qualitative research, feel free to skip Chapter 3, unless of course you need ammunition to sell the idea to your staff, CSE, or board. Other than, skipping Chapter 3 would be a mistake.

Everyone should have the opportunity to succeed. If you **follow the steps laid out** in this book and resist the urge to pick-and-choose or skip steps, you will succeed. Similar to baking a cake and skipping the baking soda, taking shortcuts greatly reduces your chances for success. Everything in this book is do-able and will deliver the desired results if you follow the steps.

You will find a URL address at the end of each chapter in the executive action steps. I have uploaded **video segments** about the chapter and would highly recommend that you take the time to watch the "bonus material." The videos might be just what you need to help sell the ideas to the skeptics in your organization.

There are different ways to attract members, keep them engaged and secure their renewal. In this book you will gain some insights into them, along with my perspectives on what works best. Since not every strategy will work the same for every group, I'll share my perspectives on the advantages that may apply to your situation.

As Phil Russo, Executive Director at NAFA Fleet Management Association said after spending a day together at his board of directors meeting, "It was the dynamite that **broke up the log jam**, now I can get to work doing my job."

The key goal of this book is to share a truly unique perspective in member recruitment and retention—one that will clearly help you to break up your member recruitment and retention log jam. Here's what's in this book for you:

Chapter 1, Examines the benefit to your organization in knowing *The ROI of Membership* in real-dollar numbers. These member-generated real-dollar numbers will become the cornerstone of your membership value proposition and member recruitment marketing collateral materials.

Chapter 2, Helps you understand the difference between member-only and industry stakeholder benefits. The chapter also explains why attempting to sell industry stakeholder benefits is generally a no-sale in member recruitment.

Chapter 3, Explores research methods for effectively getting *The ROI of Membership* numbers you need. Quantitative or qualitative methodology—you select.

Chapter 4, How to use a structured methodology for determining member ROI so all features of membership valuations are consistent within your organization. The chapter takes you through the steps of the qualitative research method—a kind of behind-the-scenes peek. Here you will find the member ROI formula. This will give you a clear understanding of how to actually get the research process done.

Chapter 5, Provides actual member-determined value averages in real dollar numbers for the most common listed and valuated features of membership. These numbers were culled and summarized from over a decade (2001-2012) of results from the *Rigsbee Member ROI Valuation Process™* qualitative research. Sessions were conducted across North America in both large and small organizations, with membership models of both individuals and companies. In the four key sub-value areas, the yearly sustainable real-dollar value associations and societies delivered to their members, on average, was:

- Professional Development...$3,944
- Business Solutions...$7,153
- Knowledge Management...$2,430
- Networking...$2,764

Chapter 6, Addresses association executive, staff, and volunteer selling skills and buying motives that drive potential members to a "*Yes*" decision. Add this understanding with the knowledge of benefits contrasted with features and your electronic and print marketing copy will sell, sell, and keep selling.

Chapter 7, Is an absolutely essential read for everyone. Skip Chapter 3 if you are already sold on qualitative research but do not fail to read this last chapter. This is the final puzzle piece—it covers the three basic member recruitment models, including why the member-get-a-member model is preferred for many organizations and show you how to create your own organic grassroots member recruitment campaign. You will truly learn how to turn current members into ***Member Recruitment Evangelists*** with the ammunition they need to make a difference.

How this Member ROI Measuring Came About

Serendipity struck when the California Alarm Association (CAA) invited me to present their conference keynote, based on my new book (at the time), *PartnerShift—How to Profit from the Partnering Trend*. The annual meeting was held on December 7, 2001 at the Sir Francis Drake Hotel in San Francisco. The organization's executive director, Jerry Lenander, asked me if I'd mind also conducting an industry roundtable discussion following my keynote.

At this meeting, the value of membership in the CAA was top of mind. I started asking questions about the features of membership and listed them on the flip chart. After we were certain the list of features was complete, I started asking questions about the value of the features in dollar numbers. This is where it got difficult for the attendees.

Next, I started explaining to the audience members various ways they could determine the value in real dollar numbers. This went on, member-only feature after feature. When we were done, I asked an attendee to add up all the numbers to get a total dollar membership value. Then I asked what it cost to be a member. We all saw it simultaneously, *The ROI of Me*mbership. Our roundtable session time was about up and everyone was happy with the work we had done.

As the CAA members were leaving the room, I looked back at the work on the flip chart and decided to take along the pages as my interest was piqued. A few days later I called the CAA Executive Director, Jerry, and told him about our work and offered to write an article for him about the real-dollar *ROI of Membership* at CAA. To my knowledge, this article was the first in association publications detailing the yearly real-dollar *ROI of Membership* numbers—as determined by members.

Quite by accident, I found myself conducting active focus group qualitative research—wow! During the years since, I have continued to improve my methodology for interaction and facilitation in search of an ROI treasure map that delivered. The result today is a credible methodology that I have named the *Rigsbee Member ROI Valuation Process™* for determining the yearly sustainable real-dollar value of membership.

This is the actual example of *The ROI of Membership* that the CAA group determined, that amazing day in San Francisco:

- $1,000 for industry specific technical training offered twice a year.
- $1,000 for business, management and marketing training twice a year.
- $300 for monthly legislative updates.
- $1,000 for coupons for goods and services offered by the national organization with national and regional membership.
- $600 for legal seminars offered twice a year.
- $200 networking value at semi-annual meetings.
- $300 tax savings on income spent attending vacations (meetings).
- $500 for mentoring opportunities available through meeting attendance.
- $200 for product knowledge gained at meetings.

- $200 for company credibility and image associated with membership.

- $300 for education in accessing local publicity.

- $200 for publicity and exposure through association membership.

During our hour session, the members in attendance came up with their membership value in real dollar numbers at $5,800.

I asked the members how much it costs them to belong to the association and attend the association's annual or semi-annual meetings. They stated that it was approximately $1,600. We determined members got on the average, $3.63 back in real-dollar value for every dollar they invest in membership: 3.6X *ROI of Membership.*

As you turn the upcoming pages, you will discover some exciting new ideas, affirmations of the great job you are already doing and a friendly nudge now and then—urging you to grow your membership by proving the ROI you already deliver. One never knows, like at the Sir Francis Drake Hotel in San Francisco, that December day in 2001 what opportunity might be ready to emerge from the unexpected. I wish you and your organization the absolute very best.

Ed Rigsbee
Thousand Oaks, California
March 2014

Chapter 1

Why Organizations Should Know Their Real-Dollar ROI of Membership

Nothing is more effective for influencing the decision to join than proving The ROI of Membership and communicating to non-members, through real-dollar numbers, that membership is a smart career, business, and/or financial decision. This is the missing link for explosive growth. This applies universally to all membership organizations—regardless of which member recruitment approach is employed—methods ranging from member-get-a-member, Internet marketing, traditional postal mail-out marketing, event marketing, hybrids and other methods.

For organizations that excel at member recruitment, this book provides the proverbial grinding stone for sharpening the axe. If you are an executive, staff person, or volunteer leader at this kind of an organization, even you will be challenged with the intent to improve. However, if you are involved with an organization that is stagnant, bleeding or even hemorrhaging members, this book will be your comprehensive guide for completely reversing your situation.

For any organization to achieve explosive growth, they must excel both at offensive (recruitment) and defensive (retention) implementation strategies. Today's missing link, *The ROI of Membership* real-dollar numbers, helps any organization to better achieve both. A recent 2014 member engagement survey (quantitative research) conducted by Vertical Leap Consulting, Icimo, LLC, and Potomac Core Consulting reveals the five top reasons why members leave both professional societies and trade associations:

1. Insufficient perceived value (ROI)
2. Retired, changed companies, in transition
3. Joined for a one-time purchase discount (e.g. meeting registration)
4. Acquired by another company that won't pay the dues
5. Insufficient connection to their business and/or professional objectives

Revealed to you in the coming pages are answers for all the reasons with the exception of number two. ROI is at the top of the list. Proving and communicating *The ROI of Membership* is core to all the solution strategies that are offered to you. If you are truly tired of going back to your core members and pleading with them to reach out to new potential members while you watch membership numbers slide, realize that the nature of membership is evolving toward a "what's in it for me" model.

If your organization is trying to sell non-members what they already can get for free, the strategy is ineffective, at best. The non-members in your industry, those that have not yet made the buying decision to join, as industry stakeholders still enjoy value from some of your organization's efforts without investing a penny. This strategy needs a major overhaul.

Everyone talks about member ROI, generally conceding that it is impossible to measure, reverting to "membership is priceless." Repeating the words that Glenn Tecker wrote in the foreward—*"This book is a truly groundbreaking work. It is different from any other 'member recruitment' book available today. It offers both strategy and tactics for proving the ROI of membership, in real dollar numbers."* In the coming pages you will receive the measurement processes you need to explain a credible ROI value proposition to the industry partakers you want to influence to join.

Priceless is Not a Member Recruitment Strategy

Priceless is great for MasterCard commercials, but not a member recruitment strategy. Priceless is a word used to describe membership when one has absolutely no idea as to the value they receive. It doesn't have to be that way. Your organization and members can do better.

To be valuable to your members, and potential members, your organization must tell them exactly how many dollars in value they should expect to receive for every dollar they invest in membership. The majority of the 50+ organizations studied by Rigsbee Research, the organization for which this author is president, delivered an average *ROI of Membership* ranging from $5 to $20 of real-dollar value returned for every dollar invested in membership.

Of particular interest are a couple of the higher standouts: the United States Hispanic Chamber of Commerce whose valuation process revealed the member ROI was $185 in value returned for every dollar invested and American Society for Quality revealed (from a three-year study) their member ROI is $50 returned for every dollar invested. These associations aren't "Priceless;" they are proven "Valuable!"

You Say Employers Aren't Paying Anymore?

For associations and societies in a number of industries, this has become an honest issue. Companies that had traditionally paid the membership dues for their employees are backing away with their resources. Consolidations have also had a similar effect—two or more companies merge and the finance people are asking why in earth everyone needs to be a member.

Not everybody is willing to accept this; however the issue is not resources but rather priorities. Companies have the money but the executives do not see the value in membership. It simply gets back to proving *The ROI of Membership.*

The Society of Government Meeting Professionals (SGMP) realized this was an issue for their members. The various government departments started asking planners to justify the cost of their dues in SGMP. A qualitative research focus group was conducted at their annual meeting, from the main stage with about 300 participants, in Nashville (2004). They learned that the members receive $21,900 in annual quantifiable real-dollar value for an investment (dues and cost of attending the annual convention) of about $2,000. The planners could then tell their employers that they received $10.95 in actual value for every dollar invested in membership and attending the annual convention. The planners could prove that membership was a smart decision. Figure 1 lists the actual valuation numbers from that session.

$5,000	Networking	$5,000	Ideas for saving my organization money
$3,000	Working with suppliers who understand my needs	$1,000	Ability to see speakers live without additional travel
$1,000	Continuing education	$1,000	Opportunities to volunteer Nationally (Development of leadership skills)
$1,000	Educational scholarships	$800	Personal and professional growth/confidence
$500	CMP and CHSP training	$500	Qualifying Continuing Education Units
$500	Mentors (Recommendations and referrals from other planners	$500	Trade Show
$500	Organization's website	$300	Support of the National organization
$300	Reimbursement for CMP training	$300	Membership directory
$200	Opportunities to see other parts of the world	$200	Recognition and awards
$200	Great parties	$100	National magazine

Figure 1

This valuation is not an indication of what your organization's numbers might be, but rather to help you with the idea that employers will pay for membership if the value can be clearly demonstrated. Price is never the issue, it is always value.

The Right Tools

Not to get ahead of ourselves, but your members need the right tools for the right job. In order to sell the value your organization delivers, you will want to produce a different kind of member recruitment brochure that "dazzles with brilliance." It will be succinct, compact, and based on *The ROI of Membership* numbers. This brochure will list the actual services and dollar value of each feature of membership offered by your organization, similar to the above SGMP profile. Details on the development are outlined for you in Chapter 7. This helps your current members to truly become active advocates, hopefully even evangelists, for the association rather than just passive members. Give them the right tools, and people will amaze you with their results.

State the ROI

Membership organizations could and should state *The ROI of Membership* they deliver, but many do not. Fear and inflexibility are generally at the root of their resistance. Reasons for not stating ROI include:

1. Unwilling to dedicate the time and/or financial resources to determine *The ROI of Membership.*

2. Afraid that if they go through the process that they will fall short of member expectations.

3. Stuck in the 1970-1980s mentality that industry stakeholders *should* join.

4. Still believe that the association is the one and only repository of industry-specific knowledge and education.

5. Still believe that 12 magazines and an annual meeting each year is enough value for members to remain loyal.

6. The Board of Directors and the paid professional staff cannot agree on the strategic direction of the organization, thereby stifling innovation and forward thinking.

7. The individuals who make up the Board of Directors are highly engaged in the organization and see the

> value they receive. They cannot fathom that others might not see the same value. Since they cannot see their organization through the eyes of the non-members, they are clueless to the need to prove *The ROI of Membership.*

Moving forward, the nature of membership, what members value and believe to deliver real-dollar ROI will naturally evolve. New ideas and technologies will create new opportunities for membership organizations to lead the value revolution, or to lag behind and dwindle into the sunset.

Associations Morphing Into Communities of Reciprocity

Twenty-first century associations desiring to survive and grow will transcend themselves beyond the 1970s and earlier paradigm of one size fits all—12 magazines and an annual meeting, into vibrant communities of reciprocity (further detailed in Chapter 5) for various member contingencies, developing relevancy for all ages and demographics of membership. A great example is the Los Angeles County Bar Association. The organization created a *Dinosaur Group* specifically for the senior lawyer members. They charge a little extra and deliver special age and topic specific meetings of interest to that community.

At the time of writing, the free (to the user) social media platforms including LinkedIn, Twitter, and Facebook offer very low-cost methods for organizations to deliver community-specific value to members. For most membership organizations, LinkedIn should be the number one choice in "free" social media platforms because of ease of use, ability to create closed groups and most business leaders participate at this platform. LinkedIn groups cost basically nothing but (employee and/or volunteer) time and deliver amazing return. It is highly recommended that groups are *closed.* The organization controls group membership. The commonly stated idea of letting everyone in for the sake of promoting and advertising the organization (aka content marketing), is counterproductive to delivering member-only ROI. If an organization's communities are open regardless of holding membership in the organization, the communities are **not** features of membership (member-only) but value available at no charge to all industry stakeholders.

Associations Competing with Google

Online information is readily available to nearly everyone. Since it is impossible for today's associations to be the exclusive holders of all industry information, best practices, building and regulatory codes, and so forth, associations must prove their value to retain members and to recruit members. The stakeholders in your industry can get much industry-specific information they need to succeed in business through a simple Google search of the topic, and they can do it anywhere with their tablet or smartphone.

This truly changes the member recruitment game. Today's "member to non-member" conversation about recruitment revolves around the idea of explaining why it is a smart career, business, or financial decision to join the association. The discussion of return on investment of resources (time and money) is important. An explanation of how the organization's work in *Knowledge Management* (how the organization stores, organizes and makes industry-specific information easily available to members) delivers the benefit of time and money savings—as a feature of membership—can be quite persuasive in helping non-members to make the decision to join.

Know the Players—Two Important Emotional Categories of Association Members

For member recruitment and retention, understanding the two basic human perspectives should be helpful in your decision to prove *The ROI of Membership.* This is an idea that has been incorporated into Rigsbee Research workshops and articles since the year 2000.

Most membership organizations can give and receive value, to and from, both categories if the members' motives are understood. With a focus on exchange in value between member and organization, remember that for some value might be receiving warm and fuzzy accolades while for others, hard-dollar ROI is top-of-mind.

First, there are the **Givers**, the people that will belong to their industry association or society and support it with attendance—no matter what. They will attend marginal meetings year after year and sing the praises. They will accept very little member-only value from their organization and keep paying their dues. Association executives everywhere are bemoaning the reality that these *jewels* are steadily vanishing. Some might say that this group is driven by ego—however that really is not the case. This group firmly believes in the idea of participation for the good of the order—meaning the good of the industry as a whole.

The second category is the **Takers**. While some might consider the term "Taker" as a negative, it need not be seen in that light. Their perspective is a simple one of business, "I'll come and play if you can show me that I will get more out than I put in." Your organization should be able to accommodate this need. This person generally tends to be either younger in age or early in their career. Many times the situation is that this person has taken over the business and views things from a managerial perspective versus the entrepreneurial perspective of the person who started it. Even if their predecessor participated in the industry association, they might not see the organizational membership value in a similar light. Their life is busy and they do not want to waste their time. To many, membership is just *networking.*

In order to successfully recruit the **Takers** into membership, your organization must clearly demonstrate that there is real-dollar value to be had. Being able to prove the ROI your organization offers will help this **Taker** to prove to him/herself that membership is a very smart business decision.

The Associated Food & Petroleum Distributors (AFPD) in West Bloomfield, Michigan has this one, **Taker Value**, tuned to perfection. The reason for about 60+% of their members joining, and the fact that the organization has enjoyed approximately 500 new-members a year (during the prior five years at time of writing) is for their vendor programs. In many ways, this program is similar to belonging to a buying group, offering generous rebates to members on their purchases from participating vendors. President/CEO, Auday Peter Arabo says, "When the economy is bad, our members need us even more." That is so much more encouraging than the other side of the coin, the association executives that explain loss of membership in bad times because membership is the first (unnecessary) expense that members cut.

ROI Numbers Necessary for All Recruitment Campaigns

Member-get-a-member campaigns, along with other approaches, are awesome provided that they are positioned correctly. Giving cash prizes, trips, and other incentives in any type of recruitment campaign is not the way to run an effective long-term membership retention organization. You want members, not numbers.

When there is any kind of financial incentive involved in member recruitment campaigns, the likelihood of competitive number-driven recruitment is higher than quality-driven. This creates a situation where the likeliness for new member retention and longevity is dramatically diminished. This generally creates a member turnstile which hurts your association in the long-term. New members recruited because of some kind of competition are less likely to receive mentorship or any kind of relationship from their recruiter. As such, the new member experiences little value or did not get the same incentive to re-join. If they do not renew, which is very likely, there is a strong chance that they will bad mouth the organization within their industry due to the lack of perceived value from membership.

Each member only recruits one

The better positioning approach is singular annual recruitment—each member only recruits one person/company a year into membership. This enables the recruiting member to be of service to the recruited member, increasing the chance of retention. Additionally the member should be recruited based on the value they could expect to receive from membership rather than pressure of any sort or incentive.

You want members, not numbers

Hopefully by the time you finish this book, you'll agree with the opening statement. Nothing is more effective for influencing the decision than proving membership is a smart career, business, and financial decision. This is achieved through proving the membership return on investment (ROI) in actual real-dollar numbers.

Chapter 1 Executive Action Steps:

1. As you read through this book, focus on three important areas:
   a. See your organization through the eyes of the non-member.
   b. Talk about how the features of membership deliver real-dollar benefit members.
   c. Understand and embrace the importance of member ROI measurement.

2. Go to LinkedIn and search groups for: *Member ROI for Associations and Societies.* Started in January 2010, this is a closed group for association/society executives and staff. If you are such a person, join the group to get an idea of how your organization can create a specific community of reciprocity for your members. As of this writing, the group is comprised of over 2,100 association executives and staff.

3. If this gets you excited about determining your own ROI profile and real-dollar numbers, start by getting a copy of this book for every Board of Directors member you need to *get on-board.* You might also consider using this book as part of your yearly board member orientation.

4. Visit www.rigsbee.com/roi1.htm for a video chapter review and additional ideas from the author.

Chapter 2

Member-Only Reigns Supreme

Who benefits from your organization's good works? Trade associations and professional societies deliver value or benefit through activities, services, and products to everyone in their industry or profession. First is the value or benefit from the features of membership that an individual or company receives. These are considered to be "member-only." The second kind of value or benefit is that which all industry members or stakeholders receive simply by being part of that industry or profession. Understanding the difference between the two is core to *The ROI of Membership* and moving your organization toward explosive growth. It is crucial that you do more than just read the chapter; you must catch its significance.

You want to deeply explore the idea of member-only benefit. Additionally, you want to have an emotional ownership in the idea of member-only as applied to your organization. This member-only concept might cause a conundrum of thought, but be assured that if you proceed carefully throughout the book—it will eventually make total and irrefutable sense. As you proceed in this chapter, the terms "value" and "benefit" are essentially interchangeable. In Chapter 6 there is a detailed discussion of the difference between feature and benefit for purposes of membership recruitment and marketing activities.

In member recruitment, the primary concept that you must understand is **member-only benefit**, because that is what is on the mind of the non-member. It's the old "What's in it for me?" Trying to convince an individual or company to invest in membership, just to get the benefit of your good works that they are already getting for free is just plain nonsense.

Your organization's efforts and achievements in some areas, like advocacy and legislative work, generally deliver value or benefit to everyone in the industry regardless of their of their membership status. This is the antithesis of member-only. These kinds of activities are not your best choice to lead off with in electronic or printed member recruitment marketing materials where you are attempting to clearly demonstrate *The ROI of Membership.*

The primary concept that you must understand is member-only benefit

Don't Get Lost in the Weeds

For years, the idea of member-only value has not always been received with the open ears, open minds, and open arms of association executives. Because the majority of associations and societies are very good at their advocacy and legislative work, there is great resistance to the idea that this as a reason to join is so frequently a "no-sale" in the minds of non-members. These organizations work hard to affect legislative action or inaction in ways that deliver positive results to their members—and generally everyone else in the industry. Since the benefits of those positive results are also enjoyed by non-members operating in the industry as well—trying to sell this as a feature of membership simply does not work in the vast majority of situations.

In this book you will **not** read the statement, "Stop your advocacy and legislative work" or read recommendations to stop other important industry specific activities that deliver value or benefit to all. Instead, arguments will be presented for increasing the member-only activities, products, and services that deliver features of membership that are highly valued by savvy individuals or companies in your industry.

While many of your long-time members might see these "value to all" activities as their member benefits, which is perfectly fine. However, this will rarely be the case with non-members. The value challenge for today's membership organizations is that everyone, regardless of their membership status, receives the benefit of some of your activities. Countless organizations are facing this debilitating conundrum daily.

To solve this challenge you need to consider, if your organization does participate in a number of value for all activities, how are you going to demonstrate member-only value or benefit? If there is a situation where your members, perhaps in the area of legislative work, get a seat at the decision making table that is the feature of membership rather than the legislative work itself.

You cannot sell guilt—that "good of the order" strategy died a long time ago. If you cannot, for example, sell the idea of a seat at the decision making table, it would be far better for your member recruitment efforts to simply put this kind of activity on the bottom of the reasons to join list. A more effective strategy would be to talk more about the activities, services, products and discounts that are member-only—available only through membership. For explosive growth, you have to sell non-members on the features of membership that they are not already getting. Skip the "good of the order" admonishments.

Surely your "benefit to all" or "industry stakeholder benefit" work will be understood to many current members and received as important activities for member ***retention***. There is no question that scores of people and organizations hold membership in associations and societies to support their political and business perspectives. However, this is rarely enough stand-alone value to convince a person or organization to join. An exception might be found in very few specific situations where impending legislation or inaction will have a paradigm changing effect, positive or negative, on the industry. An additional situation might be where membership provides valuable early warnings and opportunities to take advantage of this change. This phenomenon happens in very few industries or professions on a regular basis except those that are heavily regulated or those newly experiencing regulation.

There are many ways that this challenge can be turned around. For today's cutting-edge organizations, *Knowledge Management*, as a feature of membership, can easily be an important membership incentive. Knowledge Management is how an organization collects, maintains, uses, and makes available for member easy access—industry knowledge and information. It is all about how timely and easy your organization makes it for members to gain access to the information they need. Without effective knowledge management, your organization is competing daily with Internet search engines like Google. Unfortunately too many organizations are giving away their knowledge in the hope that non-members will use the information and join. This is a pipe dream. This is a feature of membership killer. If the non-member has not joined by now—they're not going to. **Give away only the headlines**, but not the content. By making your organization's knowledge management efforts available only to members, you can move this feature to the member-only column. Now you have a member-only feature that will influence the decision to join. This concept will be discussed in later chapters.

You have to sell non-members on what they are not already getting, as opposed to "good of the order" admonishments

The Wrong Perspective

More than likely, you have read in various contemporary association management books that you need to change. While you know this is true, some association board members, executives or staff, have erected mental brick walls so they need not see the harsh realities of the marketplace. This is where consciousness and competency intersect. Here are the progressive stages of knowledge competency:

1. **Unconscious incompetent:** Many start out in association management or leadership as an unconscious incompetent; truly having no idea of how much they don't know.

2. **Conscious incompetent:** The next stage is becoming a conscious incompetent. This is where one realizes just how much one does not know.

3. **Conscious competent:** One generally becomes a conscious competent in the mid-level stages of learning and knowledge gathering, when one comes to the realization that they know and understand. With some thought and focus they can achieve most tasks.

4. **Unconscious competent:** After an extended period of time in pursuit and acquisition of the needed education and experience one achieves the status of unconscious *competent.* At this point one simply knows what they know and does what they do without thinking or forethought. They just know and do.

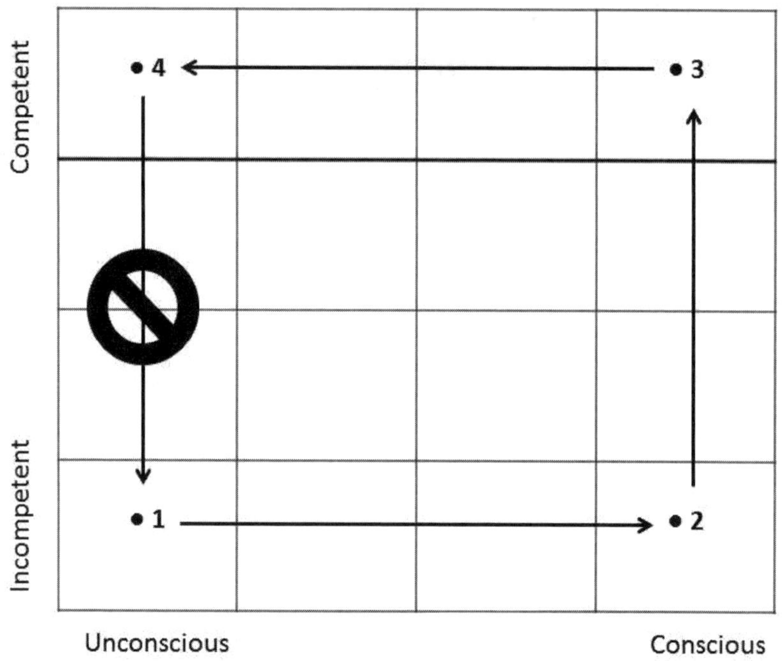

Figure 2

Land Mine in the Making

The unconscious competent can easily move from position 4 back into position 1, the unconscious incompetent. This can happen over time for the association executive, staff member or volunteer leader who chooses not to continually learn and grow by exploring new and different association management approaches. As illustrated in figure 2, when a person has the mindset of "I already know it all" unconscious incompetence can quickly follow. This is not a good thing.

Over time, discoveries are made and industries shift, thereby forcing unwanted change. Also, innovations in technology drive new methodologies—both for production and management. Simply put, stuff happens. Consider Baby Boomer association executives. Just think how much has changed during their careers.

Throw all of the above into the figurative food processer: what comes out? If you've been in the association management business for most, or all, of your career—stop for a moment at your organization's conference and listen—truly *hear* what is being discussed. Most executives are scarcely even in the room during their own conference. Do more than wander the halls at your state or national society of association executives meeting. Young presenters that are so easily dismissed sometimes have great ideas and concepts. You cannot get a true industry picture simply by attending your board meeting—the sampling is just too limited.

An excellent example of an unconscious "competent" association executive backsliding into unconscious "incompetence" is a recent interview in an associative executive publication. A CEO with twenty-five years of service was highlighted. His organization is a trade association with $9 million in revenue. The CEO is off the mark. He was asked a question regarding younger professionals' reduced association-joining mentality. His exact answer follows:

> *This is a big issue for the association community because the value proposition has changed. It used to be people joined out of an obligation almost or because all their colleagues were members and they wanted to see their colleagues two or three times a year. Now the question we get asked all the time is,*

> "What do I get for my dues?" *And it's the wrong question.*
>
> *We haven't been able to reshape the question yet, but the question should be,* "If I join the organization, how do we work together to effect change?" *Somehow we need to get our members to ask that question instead of asking,* "What do I get for my dues?" *If we reduced to that, what they get is a commodity. They get a magazine, they get information, they get access to some information they might not otherwise get, but if we commoditize information, in the long run we lose.*
>
> *In a way members are buying access to information, to expert help, but that's not worth $2,000, $3,000 or $4,000 a year. That's a very hard sell. What we're selling is intangible stuff. We're selling,* "We're going to be your voice in Washington, and we're going to be your voice before the building code community and we're going to fight for you whatever the fight is. We're going to be the advocate."

The identity of this trade association CEO is not important, however his outdated thinking is. Too many chief staff executives still see the world through the above filter and that hinders their member-only benefit understanding. If the above organization excelled in member-only knowledge management, that feature of membership would easily be worth $4,000 a year to its members, even though the CEO cannot see it.

From the 2001-2012 Rigsbee Research survey already mentioned in the Preface, it was revealed that the annual national average for the Knowledge Management category as a "feature of membership" is $2,430. For many, that could be a strong start for convincingly answering the question, "What do I get for my dues?" In Chapter 5 you will find an extensive list of additional features of membership and the, member-determined, annual average dollar value to further answer this question.

In the above example, the CEO is clearly clinging to past success but, unfortunately, still does not emotionally realize that few Generation X or Y professionals will purchase through membership what they are already getting for free, his advocacy in Washington. This CEO clearly does not understand the difference between member-only benefit and industry stakeholder benefit.

Industry Stakeholder Benefit

All of your organization's activities that deliver benefit to your industry at large, regardless of holding membership in your organization are industry stakeholder benefit. Examples might include advocacy, website content access, social media group access, and weekly/monthly publications...just to name a few. Generally the value proposition of these benefits is not sellable to non-members. In your recruitment efforts, these items will be a no-go in convincing non-members to join your organization. Non-members are already enjoying these benefits for free. The extremely tired and generally ineffective, "*support your industry*" argument will most almost certainly be lost on non-member groups, companies or individuals that get the benefits for free—but you already knew that.

Member-Only Benefit

The products, services, and discounts that your members receive by virtue of paying for their membership are the true *member-only features* that your organization delivers. These *member-only* features are going to form your organization's unique value/selling proposition tools. While non-members do enjoy the industry benefit that your organization delivers, it is the *member-only* features package that will potentially motivate the non-member in your industry to cut a check and join your organization. For effective recruitment, sell the *member-only* features and not the industry stakeholder benefits.

In Chapter 5, we'll cover the idea of your organization giving away *member-only* features—which is crazy. The thinking behind giving away value is to let non-members experience what they are missing and perhaps they will join. If they have not joined by now, they are not going to. On the other hand, employing the sampling method used by Costco, Starbucks and many others, offering small samples is fine. This method depends on giving away *just a taste* so their customers can briefly experience the product to help them make a buying decision. If you must, go ahead and **give away only the headlines**—but not your in-depth content. For that, insist on them being dues paying members.

For effective recruitment, sell the member-only features

Is Your Website Recruiting?

When developing your organization's website strategy, you must first determine who you are actually selling to. Is your "Benefits" page targeted for member recruitment or member retention? If for member recruitment, you need to introduce member-only benefits first and follow with industry benefit. If it is primarily for member retention, then simply listing the features of membership and leading with your advocacy work might be enough.

Your next consideration if you want your page to recruit members is to determine whether you are simply listing features of members and expecting prospective members to make the benefit translation for themselves or are you listing the actual benefits—how the feature makes their life better? You will learn the difference in Chapter 6.

Getting Them to Join and Stay

Frequently, when association members are asked about the value they receive from their membership they simply stumble and have no real answer. On the other hand, you feel fabulous if all the members of your association answered, *"I'd be foolish not to belong to my industry's association and participate."*

This is not always the case. An American Society of Association Executives study that was reported in the November 2001 issue of the *Association Management* magazine (renamed *Associations Now*) revealed this about the opinions of non-renewing members. Of members who did not renew, 73% was due to lack of perceived membership value. Since this study was published there have been a number of others from various organizations with similar findings. For an example, visit www.marketinggeneral.com for one of their recent membership marketing benchmark reports.

The following specific reasons were given for association members not renewing:

- 17%: Services no longer relevant
- 17%: Dues too high
- 16%: Cannot determine
- 16%: Other
- 15%: Change of profession

- 12%: Business closed/merged
- 7%: Not enough time to use member benefits

The only valid "non-value" reason in the above list is the business closing or change of profession. All the remaining reasons loudly say, "*Not enough perceived value!*" Can you believe it, 73% of the non-renewing members stated, "*Not enough perceived value!*" as the key reason for non-renewal.

Clearly, the number one reason industry stakeholders do not join your organization is not because of the answer most given by association executives, staff, and volunteer leaders—lack of time. Rather, the true reason is perceived lack of value in membership.

Too many associations wait for a disaster to drive change, but find that they do not have the will or the resources to turn their association around. That isn't leadership. You don't have to have a burning platform to make your case for change. There are compelling business cases and survey results out there that can be leveraged to make your people aware of the dangers on inaction. There is nothing wrong with sharing potential nightmares for the sake of avoiding catastrophe. Do this, and hopefully your association doesn't have to live through such predicaments. The right information, at the right time, can create the motivation for changes—changes worth making that will foster and enable increases in member recruitment and member retention.

Of members who did not renew, 73% was due to lack of perceived membership value

Chapter 2 Executive Action Steps:

1. As of this writing, Marketing General has conducted no less than five annual membership marketing benchmark reports that effectively support the "*not enough perceived value*" analysis. Visit their website for a free copy of their current membership benchmarking survey at www.marketinggeneral.com.

2. If you are not sold on this chapter yet, reread it again until you want to tell people on an elevator ride what you have just realized about *The ROI of Membership*!

3. Visit www.rigsbee.com/roi2.htm for a video review of this chapter and additional thoughts from the author.

Chapter 3

Research Methods That Work

To determine the ***ROI of Membership*** in real dollar numbers, there are two basic research methods for measurement: quantitative or qualitative. Quality research tends to be expensive. However when designed correctly, with a structured plan for data usage, the expense is usually returned in value many times over. This is particularly true in the areas of member recruitment and member retention. If you look at the people in your industry or profession as partners—you have to understand their preferences. One of the keys to value delivery, as stated in *PartnerShift—How to Profit from the Partnering Trend* is, knowing what your partner considers as valuable and delivering that—as opposed to what you "think" they want. In delivering on member expectations, "knowing" is far superior to "thinking."

Quantitative Research

This method, for most association executives is the default for ease and comfort. Quantitative research is relatively straight-forward; ask questions and solicit responses. Tally the responses in whatever slice-and-dice method serves, reveal the sampling number and there you have it. For many applications this is the best and most cost effective method for learning opinions, participation levels, desires, and so forth. Throughout this book, there are mentions of various quantitative research surveys that serve will to help support concepts that are presented.

The down side of quantitative inquiry for determining the yearly sustainable real-dollar value of membership, even when designed properly, is that it can lack context and minimize the respondents' ownership in their answers. Think about the ownership in answers by recalling the last time you completed a typical quantitative survey. Did you simply rushed through it to finish? Were you engaged in the experience? Did you really "own" your answers? Then there is the possibility of question of confusion in understanding the questions. You might also have struggled with putting the questions into the correct context. These are some of the most obvious challenges with this method.

It is highly recommended that you use the qualitative research method for the richness in response, ownership of answers, engagement, and understanding of context from the qualitative method is what you really need to determine honest and believable ROI numbers.

Why not use technology for the Qualitative Method?

Technology is great for quantitative research; however, the reason technology fails the qualitative research process is primarily context and ownership of answers. Technology removes the risk from response. In order for an effective outcome, participants within the study must own their valuation answers. The goal is not an average of blind numbers but rather a face-to-face discussion on the actual real-dollar value received from membership in any particular organization— delivered through the features of membership. For the most effective result, qualitative research focus group or interview methodologies are on top of the list.

Quantitative research depends on raw numbers, while qualitative embraces discovery

Qualitative Research

For those that might be hesitant to embrace the qualitative method's value and validity, acknowledgement must be given to Sharan B. Merriam, author of Qualitative Research: A Guide to Design and Implementation, Jossey-Bass 2009. Her book is an incredible learning tool and her insight has greatly influenced this chapter. If the qualitative method makes you uncomfortable, read Marriam's book.

While some researchers might turn a blind eye to the validity of qualitative research, the numbers of contemporary researchers embracing the qualitative method are exponentially increasing. Quantitative research depends on raw numbers, while qualitative embraces discovery. There will always be detractors for any method; hopefully they will embrace the words of highly qualified researchers.

> *"The biggest single change in the* [research] *field during the 1970s and beyond was the introduction of qualitative program evaluations. The key difference between advocates of qualitative evaluations (Guba & Lincoln, 1981; Patton, 1997) and those who continued to assert the superiority of experiments and quasi-experiments was the qualitative evaluators' emphasis on words as a basis for the analyses in evaluations. Advocates of experiments and quasi-experiments tended to emphasize the use of quantitative techniques, often involving applications of statistics to numerical data."*

James C. McDavid, Irene Huse, Laura R. L. Hawthorn, *Program Evaluation and Performance Measurement: An Introduction to Practice,* Second Edition, Sage Publications, 2013. In addition to the early qualitative researchers mentioned above, Sharan Merriam also gives credit to Bogdan & Taylor, 1975.

In the world of membership organization research, it is important to help ensure internal validity to any study. Another, more grassroots, name for internal validity is *passing the smell test*—arriving upon numbers that are believable within a stakeholder group. Once this is achieved, the internal stakeholders can labor toward external validity employing internal data, along with injecting their own personal experiences in their member recruitment efforts.

It is important to help ensure internal validity to any study

It is commonly believed among researchers that research designs, regardless of method, are subject to bias and design dangers which can adversely affect the study results and its internal validity. Furthermore, researcher preconceptions can include beliefs, stereotypes, prejudices, cultural incompetence, etc. Either researchers or subjects can behave, intentionally or unintentionally, in a manner that can distort study findings. This is more insidious in quantitative research because (1) in quantitative research this is generally not considered and (2) qualitative researchers are keenly aware of these dangers and work diligently to overcome the challenges.

The qualitative research method seeks opinions, values and experiences from participants. This is paramount when determining the value each subject believes they receive from their membership investment. A book-length example of a basic qualitative research study that would be meaningful to association executives is *Good to Great* by Jim Collins, 2001. His work was the foundation for ASAE: The Center for Association Leadership's seminal publication, *7 Measures of Success: What Remarkable Associations Do That Others Don't*, 2006, 2012.

There's Room for Both

In quantitative research the goal as an example might be to find out the percentage of members who value their membership or the percentage of members who are engaged in the organization. Qualitative research focuses more on the members' perception of their experience.

In summary, there is room for both quantitative and qualitative research methods as associations attempt to advance their member recruitment and retention efforts. Qualitative research, for our purposes in this book, is interested in how association and society members construct meaning, how they make sense of their lives, businesses and world in conjunction with their membership experience. Qualitative research gives your members their voice. When your ROI profile and numbers rings true to your members because it reflects their understanding of the true value of membership, they will be ready to ring up other potential members with the ammunition they need to get them to join.

Qualitative research gives your members their voice.

Active Qualitative Research Focus Group Methodology

In all member-involved recruitment efforts, it is important to fuel and motivate these members with published *ROI of Membership* real-dollar numbers. When these numbers reflect the personal beliefs of members, they find the information quite motivating. For members that have become internally motivated recruiters, they easily become ***Member Recruitment Evangelists***. With this in mind, the object of the *Rigsbee Member ROI Valuation Process™* is to get high-quality data in a social context where members can consider their own *ROI of Membership* perceptions in the context of the added perceptions of other members.

This *systematic inquiry* methodology benefits the final ROI numbers by holding internal validation, or passing the *smell test*, for other members of the organization. Equally important, because sample selections are generally small, is that the researcher/facilitator must design their case study, called *the Member ROI Valuation Process*, to be emergent and flexible. The need to be responsive to changing conditions during the study is crucial for success. An example might be a challenging focus group participant—a respected senior member attempting to hijack the session. This is quite common. This person must be dealt with in a swift, but professional manner that allows the member to save face in front of peers. The facilitator might have to make adjustments to the session because of the changing environment—the problem participant.

This methodology requires the research to be conducted within a *bounded system*, meaning within a single entity association where the participants and study can be fenced in around a single unit. This could mean a state chapter; it could mean the entire national organization or it could be around a specific member segment. This effectively creates each organization as its own case study. To complicate things just a bit, some organizations have compulsory membership—with state chapters or on the other side of the coin, the national organization. This should be considered when determining the unit ROI to be measured.

There are two broad categories of qualitative research: interpretive and critical inquiry. The first, *interpretive,* strives to understand phenomenon and the meaning it has for the participants. The *Member ROI Valuation Process*™ neatly fits into this category. The second category is *critical inquiry* with a goal to critique and challenge, transform or empower. The fact is that interpretive work frequently also delivers critical inquiry as a byproduct. Through interpretive sessions, generally the organization also receives an informational critique. The organizational critique can be very helpful for the organization's transformation in features of membership improvement. This occurs as a result of the discovery of which features deliver member-only benefits and which do not.

To date, the *Rigsbee Member ROI Valuation Process*™ has seen well over a decade of scrutiny from trade associations and professional societies throughout the United States and Canada. The process has experienced a wide range of rigor in the field from resistant staff, boards of directors, and members. The system and methodology have continually been improved. What has been learned is that this process, when followed, always works and delivers believable ROI numbers every time.

This process, when followed, always works

Rejected Research

It is unfortunate; however the topic of research rejection by board members or even association executives is necessary to cover at this point. Perhaps you have experienced this yourself? In some organizations, even industries, there are self-proclaimed intellectuals and some academics that may use peer-level research standards to argue against the validity of the valuation process presented in this book or that presented by others. One association executive tells the story of how a long-time staff person threw out the results from a particular study because the method did not match his/her opinion of rigor.

You might need to create a written plan for selling your organization's staff or board members on the value of determining the real-dollar *ROI of Membership*. For the most difficult people, allow them to read this chapter. You want the process of moving your organization forward to be contagious! Good leaders don't just surprise their people with great ideas; they circle back to get people involved early to help the excitement for change to grow.

Chapter 3 Executive Action Steps:

1. Review your quantitative research response rates, question quality, and validity of answer ownership. If there is any chance of receiving flawed results...

2. Discuss with your staff what pressing questions qualitative research might better answer for your organization and consider organizing focus groups at your next member meeting or convention.

3. Visit www.rigsbee.com/roi3.htm for a video chapter review and additional ideas from the author.

Chapter 4

The Rigsbee Member ROI Valuation Process™

The Rigsbee process is a systematic outcome assessment for determining *The ROI of Membership* in yearly sustainable, real-dollar numbers. It employs both the formative and dynamically changing evaluation methods, including the execution, analysis, and application of effective focus groups. A reasonable sampling of an organization's membership is necessary. When done correctly, the result is member-generated ROI numbers that will be believable within the specific industry or profession.

Benefit of Member-Determined Numbers

Measurement using the qualitative process could be considered inexact. This might be due to possible variances from the perspective of user engagement and usage for both the current member and prospective member, and that's okay. The reality though, is that the outcome of (user) member-generated content is, in many ways magical, because your members will support that which they help to create.

Some organizations have taken a good, first step in recognizing the importance of determining the *ROI of Membership* in real dollar numbers. They have developed member benefit web pages listing the dollar value for each feature of membership—as determined by staff. Some have even developed elegant ROI calculators for their websites. While an argument could be made in favor of staff-generated numbers as staff might have more access to information about the organization's features of membership—it is the ownership and validation of the (user) member-generated data you're members will embrace.

When recruitment and retention is the desired result, the list features of membership value numbers generated from this qualitative process will be the "member-recruitment gold" for your members to truly become ***Recruitment Evangelists***.

Members will support that which they help to create

People in general, and members in specific, believe data in a particular hierarchy of credibility:

1. People listen to themselves first. User-generated data tends to be the most believable since the users created it.

2. People listen to their friends and family second. They will generally believe what their friends and colleagues have helped to create.

3. People listen to advertising last. They are suspect to data and marketing messages created by businesses, corporations, and other organizations.

With this in mind, the staff-created ROI numbers would be considered third in the hierarchy belief system. This should be taken into consideration when an organization decides to introduce an "ROI Calculator" or other instrument developed from staff-determined member ROI numbers.

Using the top of the "hierarchy" just makes sense. Your grassroots members need reliable member ROI information in order to become ***Member Recruitment Evangelists***. They will be much more confident influencing new members to join with their own numbers or even the numbers their member colleagues have determined.

Another benefit of member-determined ROI numbers is for organizations that rely on a staff-driven member recruitment model. Association staff members will find it far more effective during the recruitment process to communicate a statement like, "We have surveyed our members and they have told us that they receive X dollars back every year in real dollar value for every dollar they invest yearly in membership." This kind of a sales presentation is more convincing than one centered on value numbers determined by the headquarter staff.

What one helps to create is more likely to be remembered and repeated

Members need reliable member ROI information to become Member Recruitment Evangelists

Valuing Different Features

An important aspect to *The ROI of Membership* approach is that different people will value different features of membership, differently. If an organization relies primarily on one or two features of membership for recruitment and a prospective member is uninterested or even hostile to those features, the result will be a no-sale. However, if an organization offers a substantial list of features of membership and the average member-determined value of each feature, then the prospective member can mentally eliminate the features that are of no interest to them. Membership based on the features that are of interest to the individual or company can still add up to a figure that is substantially greater than their investment in membership.

Selling the Idea to Board and Staff

To get started on this process of real-dollar value discovery, you may find roadblocks to agreement in conducting this process at either the board or staff level, or at both. The board level may fear the research cost or revealing a sub-par real-dollar ROI. The fear of high-dues paying members discovering sub-par value delivery can be particularly worrisome—but rarely ever seen realized. As for the cost—what's the potential cost of inaction? How much has it cost the organization to be flat in the area of membership increases, or worse...membership decreases? It can be a very simple dollars-and-cents discussion: how many dollars out for how many dollars in?

Staff may feel that they, the staff, should be good enough to do it themselves. Or they may feel protective in a silo of fiefdom operation. The chief staff executive's job is to assure the staff that they are good enough, that they are valued, that there are good and justifiable reasons for using an outside facilitator and that doing so does not lessen the stature of the professional staff. A collaborative attitude goes a long way. Let the staff be part of the decision, or at minimum, part of the event. Explain to them how having the *ROI of Membership* numbers makes their "selling" job easier. Let them know that they will certainly be involved in helping the process take flight. They play a critical enabling function to help members "sell" what they have created.

Get the Correct Facilitator

Conducting the active qualitative research to determine real dollar number *ROI of Membership* requires skill. This process incorporates both art and science. Understanding the science behind, and history of, qualitative research discussed in the previous chapter is very helpful. The art is displayed through the skill of the facilitator in how he or she can create an environment where the participants truly desire to open up and actively participate.

There is no doubt that the facilitator's role is a crucial element for success and ultimate research process validity. A quality, well-trained, and experienced facilitator will deliver consistency of application to the process in how questions are asked and explanations given. In this application, the facilitation process is more important than the research design as the design is provided in this chapter.

You will discover important elements necessary for understanding how to conduct *The ROI of Membership* focus group process. This is an evolving process that has emerged from over a decade of field work and experimentation.

Get a Pro

Because the research methodology includes a dynamically changing element, an experienced facilitator will more likely have the ability to continually adjust when course-corrections are necessary, compared to a novice who might not have developed such skills. To conduct this focus group successfully and obtain the best results, you will want to select an impartial third party with highly developed facilitative skills.

Professional facilitators are your best choice. There are a number of people in your community that possess acceptable skill sets to conduct this research. A good place to start is at the website of the International Association of Facilitators; http://www.iaf-world.org.

If this option is not affordable for your organization, consider a retired executive, perhaps someone from your local SCORE? The SCORE Association "Counselors to America's Small Business" is a nonprofit association comprised of over 13,000 volunteer business counselors throughout the U.S. and its territories—348 SCORE chapters in urban, suburban and rural communities. Visit http://www.sba.gov/content/score for more information.

Another possibility that might serve your organization is to think of people in your personal network, who have been able to get the best results out of group discussions. You may already know an excellent facilitator. If all else fails, you might consider a local teacher or college professor (with the warning that their background might compel them to act more as an expert than a facilitator).

The Staff Should Not Facilitate

Any paid staff (executive or other) and volunteer officers cannot be impartial. The key is to have impartial facilitation where the facilitator's own perspective does not substantively impact, positively or negatively, on the features of membership values determined by the members. It is easy for an inexperienced facilitator to consciously or unconsciously influence the final research results.

Selecting Membership Samples

There is no question the selected participants for the qualitative research process will have a profound effect on the results, which is totally fine. For a successful result, you will want to have a minimum of about 30 members and a maximum of about 300, with 50-100 being a very effective and manageable sample size.

The discussion of numbers is important. If done correctly, a sampling of 75-100 can be quite accurate for an organization with a membership of 2,000 to 5,000. Use a random pull invitation method, participants are randomly selected from each demographic that matters to your organization such as: geography, organization employee size, revenues, length of time in business, length of time holding membership, service sector, ethnic diversity, age and sex diversity, time in the industry, and the like. Your paid professional staff should be quite capable of putting the sample group together effectively and without prejudice. Such a cross section of participants will deliver very credible results.

Consider whether a single research focus group session is adequate or if multiple sessions are required. Different groups might value a number of your features of membership quite differently. This can be extremely helpful for your organization as you move forward in an effort to understand *The ROI of Membership* and adjust the features of membership offered. You will have a better idea of what to keep, improve, and discontinue.

Various organizations have various names for membership types. There are basically two or three types of members: those actively participating in your industry, their vendors, and their customers. Frequently retired, student, and other types of members tend to be far fewer total numbers. If this is the case for your organization, their input would carry far less weight. Never eliminate your vendor, supplier, or allied members from considering the value they receive.

Vendor Value

In almost every case, it has been determined that vendors receive quite a bit more value than the active (rank and file) industry member. The accelerated value differential is all over the board depending on the industry.

A recent example is a large state contractors association in Georgia. Conducting separate valuation sessions for vendors/suppliers/subcontractors compared to the general contractors revealed that the vendors were getting just over double the real-dollar value the contractors were receiving—while paying quite a bit less in membership dues. Value information like this might cause organizations to review various category membership dues. Are they paying too much or not enough? This is a discussion worthy of exploration.

The reason for the increased real-dollar value is because the vendors are there to sell their goods and services directly to members as opposed to industry members trying to learn how to improve their business. You might want to consider conducting a separate research focus group for your vendors and regular members. The benefit to your organization of separate focus groups is the potential for realization of higher ROI value for vendors. This could help justify and lead to possible vendor membership fee adjustments.

In a 2003 valuation process for one of the national pipe distribution associations revealed the increased supplier/vendor value. After the valuation session at the annual meeting that year, one of the board members named Earle, a supplier, did his own personal member ROI valuation which was published in the organization's magazine. It revealed quite a bit more ROI for "Earle the supplier" than that of the average distributor member. This is a common occurrence.

Average Pipe Distributor Member			
$10,000	Networking/Contacts	$3,000	Tax Savings on Recreational
$2,000	Professional/Educational Speakers	$1,000	Trends Information
$1,000	Regulatory Updates	$1,000	Website Inventory
$750	State of Industry Survey	$500	New Ideas
$500	Educational Sessions	$500	Professional Image/Exposure
$200	Membership Directory	$50	Magazine
$0	Insurance/Programs		
$10,000	Total Cost of Membership	**$20,500**	Total Value of Membership

Figure 3

Supplier Board Member (Earle's) Value			
$50,000	Networking/Contacts	$20,000	Professional Image/Exposure
$5,000	New Ideas	$5,000	Website Inventory
$5,000	Educational Sessions	$3,000	Tax Savings on Recreational
$2,000	Professional/Educational Speakers	$1,000	Trends Information
$1,000	Regulatory Updates	$750	State of Industry Survey
$200	Membership Directory	$50	Magazine
$10,000	Total Cost of Membership	**$93,000**	Total Value of Membership

Figure 4

Generational Value

Dig deeper into your organization to understand the perceived value of membership. Conducting multiple research focus groups by age diversity is an excellent approach; results for Generation Y, Generation X, and Baby Boomers will be quite enlightening in determining the dollar value of your organization's member-only line item features of membership. Various features of membership might be valued differently by generation.

As an example, conducting qualitative research sessions for the American Society for Quality revealed something very interesting in the dollar number valuation for their Recognized Certifications. The Baby Boomers valued this feature of membership (per year) at $100, the Generation X group at $1,000 and the Generation Y group at $10,000. Just a few years earlier the average results from six mixed-age sessions over a three year period revealed the yearly value at $2,500. This information might cause your organization to customize marketing materials based on age groups, pushing forward what they care about most. Boomers care about moving from successful to significant while the Generation Y group is running hard just to be successful. The younger members also have more time to capitalize on the value of certification, if your organization offers it. This feature could be used as leverage for lifetime or long-term membership.

In addition to generational, multiple focus groups based on geography can serve your organization too. If your organization is international in scope, focus groups by country can deliver valuable member-only features user data. If your organization is international but a large membership segment is in a single country like the United States, then conduct a focus group for the large member country (USA domestic) and one for all others (international).

Boomers care about moving from successful to significant while the Generation Y group is running hard just to be successful

Gathering Sample Groups

There are two basic approaches to gathering your sample group: invited and random. The random approach works well at annual conventions, expos, and meetings. With a large number of members in attendance, and if you offer some kind of incentive, a good mix will generally show up. Remember that perfection is not your goal. However, passing the "smell test," the process of filtering through the empirical knowledge sensibilities of members and others, is crucial. Numbers that are pretty close are adequate for end-game application.

Reserve a couple (back-to-back) concurrent sessions on your schedule as you will need two hours to do the session well. Do this just before lunch and announce in the program that only 100 members will be admitted—and that a special lunch (something nicer than rubber chicken) will be served in the room immediately following the session. Members will turn up. Leaving it open to convention attendees can work well and be the least expensive approach to determining real-dollar member ROI. They will also be more likely to positively gossip about the experience and insights learned.

Some might argue that this is not valid because convention attendees tend to be more involved in their association and thus will value the features of membership higher. While there might be some validity to this line of thinking, there are always some newer members to the association at conventions and they will embrace this kind of inquiry, thereby balancing your membership sample.

Another approach for gathering a sample group is to do so in conjunction with offering an industry workshop, one that the association or vendors might sponsor. Adding an educational presentation to the event might be just enough incentive to get members to show up. Make it a half-day or evening event. Bring in a content expert to give the attendees a solid "how-to" workshop (one to two hours) and follow up with a two-hour "How to Get More from Your Association" qualitative research focus group session. If the staff and leadership work the phones well, and employ social media and other marketing techniques, a good number of members will turn up and stay for the whole event.

Conducting multiple research focus groups by age diversity is an excellent approach

Measure Just Member-Only Features

Once your sample group is organized, it is important to have the proper focus on what can and cannot be measured. Member-only is an important aspect of determining the yearly sustainable real-dollar value of membership. Differentiating between member-only and (free to everyone) industry benefit will help those in your organization charged with member recruitment. Your ***Member Recruitment Evangelists*** must have something to entice non-members to join—something of value, something necessary, and something the non-members currently do not receive. Your marketing materials should focus on the features of membership. Only list the industry stakeholder "benefits to all" secondary or perhaps not at all.

As you now know, member-only features are the activities, products, and services, and discounts that are only available to persons or companies that hold membership in your organization. As an example, since your legislative and advocacy work is important and considered to be a benefit to the whole industry, your legislative update is a member-only feature—as you "do not" freely distribute this to non-members. If you "do" freely distribute possible features of membership like your legislative updates, it is highly suggest you discontinue this practice immediately. From a member ROI perspective, you are shooting yourself in the foot every time you do this.

If you offer your legislative update or any product or service to members for free—or at a discount and to non-members at a higher price, then that difference measured in dollars is the actual feature of membership benefit.

Differentiating between member-only and industry benefit will help those in your organization charged with member recruitment

Conducting Your Qualitative Research

Facilitator Guidelines for Active Focus Group Method:

The facilitator and client must be realistic in their expectations of participants and their understanding of human beings in the perception and determination of personal membership value. In obtaining real-dollar ROI numbers, you are attempting to get general group consensus—not absolute group agreement. During a typical two-hour focus group, one cannot drill down to the last nickel. Remember the *Slicer and Dicer*? In the end, the most important test your ROI research numbers must pass is the "smell test"—whether it's believable or reasonable to the members and prospective members. Since the ROI numbers are member-generated as opposed to staff-generated, the numbers will generally be more believable to all the players in your industry. For most focus group sessions, it is best to plan on two-hours—without breaks.

In the end, the most important test your ROI numbers must pass is the "smell test"

Qualitative Focus Group Process Steps

I. **Pre-focus group preparation.** Start-off with the organization's features of membership already listed. The use of presentation software like PowerPoint® is preferable. This allows the real-time projection of the work for attendees to view during the entire process. Large paper tablets (flip charts) can be used, however, this method will generally prove to be difficult for participants to see and can make the process more cumbersome and time consuming. Assuming the facilitator has spent a reasonable amount of time reviewing the client's website, the facilitator can predetermine that the list only contains member-only features. This will speed things up substantially. The features should be listed **without** any dollar value attached. The features of membership lists are usually found at the association or society's website under "Member Benefits." With the features of membership list in clear view of the participants, the facilitator should explain each item quickly and then ask the attendees if there are additional member-only features that the organization offers but are missing from the list. If so, have a volunteer or pre-determined staff member input this information into the current slide projected on the screen or on the paper tablet.

II. **Explain features of membership.** Now the facilitator must clearly and succinctly explain the difference between an industry-wide value proposition delivered by the organization and a member-only benefit. An understanding of the distinction between the two is necessary because the facilitator must, even though already pre-explored, solicit information from the attendees about each feature of membership as to whether it is offered to the public or industry at no charge or an increased price. An example of this might be the member directory or legislative update. If available only to organization members perhaps in hard copy or through a password protected members-only section of the organization's website, then it is a true feature of membership. However, if an item or service is offered to non-members at no charge even though some members consider it to be valuable, then this feature is not to be considered as a member-only benefit and cannot be added. The process facilitator must remember, and continually communicate to participants, that the focus group is measuring **ONLY** those benefits that are exclusively available through membership. This is because the end-use of the determined numbers is primarily used for member recruitment purposes as opposed to member retention.

III. **Attendees add to the list.** After the attendees have exhausted exploring the additional membership feature line-items, it is time for the facilitator to transition into the process dollar valuation. It is generally best to list networking as the last feature of membership to value because this will also serve as a catch-all for dollar value not placed on any other feature. Take one item at a time and discuss the yearly sustainable real-dollar value that the attendees believe they receive on a yearly basis.

IV. **How to determine actual value.** During the actual dollar-number determination, frequently additional explanation from the facilitator will be necessary. As an example, part of the real-dollar value of an organization's legislative update is figured by the amount of time it would take a member, or their clerical staff, to amass the information critical to their business or profession that your organization already provides. In the case of one particular western area state gaming association, the legislative update feature of membership proved to provide members with over $100,000 of yearly-sustainable real-dollar value when the just "clerical" time-cost necessary to gain the information was measured.

a. Explain it this way...let's say it would take the member 20 hours a year to find and access the information that your organization spoon-feeds them. Part of the real-dollar value is 20 multiplied by the total employee/executive hourly cost (not just the hourly income) of the member or their staff person. To figure the total cost, include pay, and all expenses the company pays for that person to be there, including payroll taxes, other benefit costs and workstation/office space costs and utilities. Additionally in the ROI number, opportunity value might be added along with timely risk mitigation value—and anything else one might think applies.

V. **Multi-year value determination.** If the total dollar amount of a particular value item is generated or received by a member or members over a number of years, have them divide the amount by the number of years the value was received. This delivers an average yearly dollar number that is very honest. An example of this might be the "Opportunity to Serve in Leadership" within the organization. For many a member, this can be similar to "figuratively" receiving an MBA—or at least a great part of the MBA business and organizational knowledge. Ask attendees what this kind of education would cost at an institute of higher learning. What would an MBA cost? What would several classes cost? Divide that by how many years the person has been a member and that would be the yearly sustainable real-dollar value of the participating in leadership as a feature of membership.

a. With the above example, remember to add the value of real-time learning from peers. Also add the real experience in making leadership/management mistakes as an association leader will never be as costly as doing the same at one's own business or company. Doing so at a company might be a career ender. Ask what the average lag time is in the group's industry for an executive to find a new job. Ask the average pay and determine a total dollar number that can be added to the above education number and then divide by years in the association or society. Now you have an honest feature of membership number.

b. It can be a negotiation. For each member-only feature there could be extended argument about the numbers; this is where the facilitator must engage his or her skill and bring the attendees to general consensus. Give the challenging people time to be heard but do not let them hijack the meeting by sharing their opinion for too long. The facilitator must keep the process moving or the vast majority of participants will mentally check-out.

c. Complete agreement is not absolutely necessary. Rather, a general consensus number that is close and reasonable—one that is not too high or too low would be selected. If the majority (approximately 75% is a good barometer) say the dollar-value number is X, then go with X.

VI. **Zero is acceptable.** It is perfectly fine if some items are valued at zero dollars. This might be because that feature is, in actuality, an industry value or it might be a zero value because the majority of members do not take advantage of the particular product or service. This frequently happens in the case of valuing an organization's affinity programs. Do not worry about the zeroes; it helps the process pass the "smell test" that builds trust in the final numbers. At the end of the session, the facilitator can suggest those items be placed on the agenda for the next board of directors meeting. This is a great opportunity for the board to conduct a value audit of the line-items listed as zero.

VII. **Multiply per employee.** The value attributed to some of the features might need to be multiplied by the number of employees in the case of company memberships as opposed to individual memberships. For some features like opportunities for involvement in leadership, educational seminars, and safety programs—just to name a few—the value "per participating employee" must be added to the total for any particular feature of membership where it applies.

VIII. **Calculate the numbers.** When all the actual features of membership have been determined and assigned a dollar number by the focus group, add them up for a total value real-dollar number. Add this number into the current slide. Next, determine the cost of membership and list it on the slide. Then divide the cost number into the value number to get the multiple of ROI and list it on the slide.

a. Remember these numbers are annual. As an example, the total annual, features of membership value is $50,000 and the annual cost of membership is $5,000. By dividing $5,000 into $50,000 one would end up with 10. This would be the ROI multiplier...10X yearly ROI. The member is getting $10 back in value, each year, for every dollar invested in membership. For most, this would prove that membership is a good business decision.

b. A caveat for the calculations: If you want to include the line-item value derived through members attending the annual meeting, convention, or other activity; you must also include the cost of attendance to the cost of annual membership. Depending on the organization, using or not using the annual meeting or other activity in the calculation is acceptable. If non-members are allowed to attend meetings, then the member-only dollar value is actually just the registration discount that members receive.

How it Might Look

This actual example of a state general contractors association makes the point that for some features of membership in the case of company memberships, some features of membership must be multiplied times the number of participating employees for a grand total ROI number.

State General Contractors Association			
$7,500	Member Owned Workers' Compensation Program	$3,000	Safety Programs
$3,000	Networking	$2,500	Affinity Programs
$2,500	Young Leaders **(possible per employee)**	$2,000	Peer Referrals
$2,000	Opportunities for Involvement & Leadership **(per employee)**	$2,000	Prestige and Recognition through Awards
$1,500	Peer Support/Mentoring	$1,500	Access to Association Office & Staff
$1,000	Convention and Conference Tax Deduction Travel Benefit **(per employee)**	$500	Forum eMail
$500	National Organization Store	**$300**	Educational Seminars **(per employee)**
$100	Membership Directory	$100	Legislative Day
$5,000	Total Cost of Membership	$30,000	Total Value of Membership

Figure 5

In figure 5, for an average general contracting company of 20 employees with dues of $5,000 (actual organizational average), multiply 20 employees times the per employee benefit of $3,300 (subtracting Young Leaders as only a possible benefit) for a total additional value of $66,000. Add that to the above total of $30,000 for a Grand Total of $96,000 annual real-dollar value. Divide the $5,000 dues into $96,000 for a 19.2X ROI—$19.20 in return real-dollar value for every dollar invested in membership.

$$\frac{\textit{Total Features of Membership Value}}{\textit{Cost of Membership}} = \textit{ROI of Membership}$$

Group Dynamics

About 85-95 percent of the association members in attendance at your qualitative research session will be quality people—totally engaged in discovering the collective ROI dollar number, and have the collaborative attitude. With a reasonable amount of direction, your members will work hard to deliver realistic and believable dollar value numbers that can help all concerned to better understand that membership in your organization is a smart business decision. But there will always be a small minority present, who are not willing or able to get with the program. These persons can easily derail even the most organized focus group session. One of the important skill sets for any facilitator to embody is the ability to keep a session moving at a pace that allows proper valuating while not needlessly dragging on. A "too slow" moving session can create a situation where participants disengage—or worse, become disruptive to the process. The facilitator will need to be ready for disruptions to the process.

Disruptive Personalities

The facilitative challenges in conducting this kind of qualitative research are many. Too light, or too heavy, of a hand can result in either pandemonium or withheld participation—neither serving the process well. Disruptive personalities include:

"The Senior Orator" feels it incumbent on him/herself to share, in great detail, their value perspective of every member-only and industry stakeholder benefit...along with their rationale for the member value delivered. This person can easily hijack the session if not delicately controlled. This person must be given his or her due and be heard, based on their long-term driven elevated status—and also must be controlled. Be careful, being too firm or too patronizing with this senior member may cause him/her to close down and so will a number of participants that respect this member.

Since it is better not to have breaks which cause disruption in the flow of the process, pulling aside a **Senior Orator** and encouraging them to delay their valued contributions generally is not an option. What can be done is to identify, with the help of the organization's staff, the **Senior Orators** "before" the session and appeal to their value and their help in getting more input.

> Say to them, "*Your comments will be very helpful and need to be heard, but people respect you so much it often can cause them to pause or not contribute. I sure value knowing I can count on you for valuable input, but I would appreciate it if you could hold back a little, early in the process and let more people get their thoughts out. If I need you to help get things going, I know I can look at you and you'll be there with some input we can use. Would you be willing to help me out?*"

"The Whiner" brightens a room by exiting it. However, the whining member must be included and encouraged to participate. An effective method for dealing with the whiner is the classic sales method of overcoming objections called the Feel...Felt...Found Method. This is where the researcher acknowledges the **Whiner's** (valid) feelings by stating, "I understand how you feel." Then the facilitator moves them to other similar situations to diffuse the negative energy. The facilitator continues, "In sessions like this for other organizations, some attendees have felt the same way." Diffuse the **Whiner's** complaints by describing positive outcomes that have been found. For example: "At X organization they found out that they were getting Y value from Z member-only feature and realized that..." Whiners, like

Senior Orators, just need to be heard. Hear them briefly, and move on quickly.

"The DNA Contrarian" is not the basic contrarian who simply sees things differently. Contrarians generally have valid opinions that may not be consistent with accepted mainstream opinions. Differing opinions in discussion generally prove to be innovatively healthy. However, the **DNA Contrarian** simply must argue for the sake of argument. This attitude is in their DNA—they just can't keep themselves from sharing a differing opinion. The facilitator must effectively control this person from the beginning of the session by standing up to them while still showing respect, or the focus group process will become nothing more than a gripe, bellyache, and complaint session. It is important for the facilitator to let this person politely know that their antagonism will not be tolerated. The facilitator can politely state something like, "Thank you for sharing." And then quickly move on.

"The Duffer" is the kind of person who might say, "It is too hard to figure out what membership is worth in real dollars." Another of **The Duffer's** favorites is, "Well, I don't know what it is worth to me." This person is different from the **Whiner**—they are just unwilling to exert the energy to engage their brain and do the work to figure out their perceived *ROI of Membership.* If coddled a bit, this person will generally come around. They will need more detailed direction than most in how to figure their value numbers. Spending just a little bit of extra time with this kind of person at the beginning can quickly convert them into a valued participant.

"The Slicer and Dicer" can turn a two-hour process into a two-day event. While this person is less common, beware. If you get a person who wants to break up every feature of membership into smaller parts (slicing and dicing) be firm and remind this person that the process is both science and art. Remind them that the goal is to create a reasonable list that can be used by the organization in a number of ways. Say something like, "For our purposes here, going too micro will derail this process and dramatically hinder your organization's member recruitment efforts."

Interview Method

A second and less recommended qualitative research approach to determine *The ROI of* Membership is the interview method. Achieving similar results to the active focus group method could be challenging. As with the focus group method, it is also not recommended for staff to conduct this research. There are two key issues with the interview method, especially if conducted by staff.

The first consideration is cost; interviewing enough members for valid findings can be time consuming and expensive when employing a professional, however the results will be superior to that of the association staff. If a C-level staff person conducts the interviews, the actual real cost to the organization will always be higher than anticipated. There is also a strong chance for interviewer bias that might be driven by the desire for favored products or serves to be valued highly by members. This could diminish the total member perceived value of the sampling.

Second is the lack of community or context. When a group of members discusses the value they receive from their membership, this discussion creates a context for understanding. Ideas and values get bounced off one another, resulting in a more authentic and believable ROI number for each feature of membership. When using a staff person to conduct interviews, as stated, interviewer bias will almost certainly play a powerful role in the results as well as losing the authentic generation of ideas from the group dynamic.

For organizations that cannot afford, or are not able to use an independent facilitator, interviews conducted by the least "organizationally entrenched" executive or staff member would be the way to go. If you desire to proceed with the interview method, consider the following:

I. The interviewer, especially if the person is an association employee or volunteer leader (which is not recommended), must keep his/her preconceived notions of the value of various features to his/herself. Any interviewer must only explain how to determine value and not influence the final line-item numbers.

II. One person, rather than several, should conduct all interviews, as this will create continuity and context. The number of interviews should range from 30-50.

III. The member sampling should include representation of all demographics including age, experience, years in the industry, business/practice size or volume, ethnicity, organizational culture and geographic diversity.

IV. The interviews should be conducted in as short a calendar time period as possible. This helps the interviewer and those to be interviewed, to remain consistent in questions and methodology.

V. Interview location(s) should be neutral, a location where neither researcher nor interviewee holds location power. The location needs to offer few distractions or disruptions.

VI. Past interview valuation numbers should not be revealed to each succeeding interviewee as this information will have a profound effect on that person's value perception. The result will be skewed data. This is the area where peer pressure in the focus group method generally harvests larger member value numbers.

VII. The same questions, in the same order should be asked during all interviews.

VIII. After all interviews are conducted, only then should the numbers be crunched. First add and average the response numbers for each feature of membership. These final averages can be used the same as with the focus group method numbers. Then add the averages for a total average ROI number response. Last, divide value by cost and you'll have your multiplier, X dollars in return for every dollar invested in membership.

What's Next After the Facilitation?

If your organization is going to invest time and money to conduct the qualitative member ROI research, take the next step and use the information in your member recruitment and retention efforts. There are three quick, easy, and inexpensive ways to use this new-found, yearly-sustainable, real-dollar *ROI of Membership* information.

1. The simple single-page, tri-fold, member recruitment brochure that will dazzle your prospects with brilliance rather than baffle them with bulk. This is your most elegant usage. The idea of mailing out pounds of paper and packaging about your organization is an obsolete concept. You know that the membership prospect will never read it all. Be smart; just give them the most important membership value proposition information. This can easily be done on one standard sheet of paper. You will find brochure creation details in Chapter 7.

2. Build a true "Benefits of Membership" web page. Too many association and society websites have a "member

benefits" page that simply list the features of membership but not the benefits that each of the features will deliver. Build a page that states, *Membership: What's In It For You?* Lead with your strength; explain how membership in your organization will make their personal and professional life better. Focus on **member-only features** and list industry features at the end. Refer to Chapter 6 for detailed information on explaining the benefits of each feature of membership.

3. If your organization mails out hard-copy membership renewals, include this new-found member ROI information. For very little cost your organization can include a page in the envelope that lists *The ROI of Membership*, feature after feature and the real-dollar value numbers. For almost no cost, simply print the information on the back of the renewal form. You can also enclose your new tri-fold member recruitment brochure to remind members of the value they receive and recommend that they pass it along to a non-member.

4. Also consider this idea: print two-sided business cards with a list of the ROI member benefit values along with association contact information and website. Encourage members to carry cards with them as a handy "evangelism" tool for their next member convert. You may even want to personalize the cards for members so that their name is there to more easily connect with a new member at their first meeting or event.

It is crucially important to remember that each year at the time of renewal; your current members must make a new buying decision. Make it easier for them to make the correct buying decision by reminding them that membership in your organization is a smart decision. Do this by reminding them of the actual real-dollar ROI they receive for their investment in membership with your organization. As long as your information was produced within the proceeding five years, it will be received as relevant by your members.

Chapter 4 Executive Action Step:

1. Decide for yourself how you want to proceed with your qualitative research focus group or interview method. Consider possible internal or external facilitators that may be able to drive the process.

2. Get the research session(s) on your organization's calendar now. Then, if necessary, immediately call your chief elected officer or chief staff officer and sell your idea. If you have already provided them with a copy of this book, it should be an easy sell.

3. Get your staff on-board by first spending some time explaining both the process and goal—perhaps even let them scan this copy of the book? Only then should you assign a staff member to implement. This will minimize the chances for your procrastination and maximize your likelihood of success. Armed with credible real-dollar ROI numbers, you can then proceed with additional recommendations that will be offered in the coming chapters.

4. Visit www.rigsbee.com/roi4.htm for a video chapter review and additional ideas from the author.

Chapter 5

Know What Each Feature of Membership is Worth

To experience explosive membership growth, know how your current members value each feature of membership offered by your organization. Then you can use this information to influence non-members to make the decision to join.

This knowledge of member perceived value will also allow your organization's leadership to make more accurate cost/value analysis of the various features of membership—helping to determine what to keep and what to abandon. For member retention and recruitment, determining and improving your organization's total value membership proposition is an essential element of success.

As already mentioned, membership in your organization is not ***priceless***. First, there is a price one must pay in order to enjoy the features of membership. Next, each of those features has, in the mind of prospective members, a possible dollar value ranging anywhere from zero to a princely sum.

When someone says that membership in their organization is ***priceless***, they are actually stating, "I have absolutely no idea of the monetary value I receive from my membership dollars." They perceive their membership as an expense rather than an investment. This is not very encouraging to a possible new member.

Similarly, on the member retention side, if your organization's members also see their membership as an expense rather than an important investment, during tough times, membership is one of the first things to go. Chances are, you've been there, seen that, and done that...no need for history to repeat itself.

In truth, there is no question that your organization delivers yearly sustainable real-dollar value to members in several areas. By encouraging your members to measure each value proposition feature by feature, they can easily see for themselves, through real-dollar ROI discovery, why membership in your organization is a good business decision for them to make and remake every year. Your members will believe and support what they help create, and hopefully become ***Member Recruitment Evangelists*** for your organization. They will work hard to convince the industry non-members to make a new decision, and join your organization.

Looking for Additional ROI in All the Right Places

A crucial tactic for determining your organization's total member-only ROI is to dig deeper into your features of membership activities, especially in the general areas of professional development, business solutions, and knowledge management. Knowledge management, for example, is an area ripe with ROI opportunity. Knowledge management is partially about creating easy and efficient access by members to industry or professional knowledge. This feature has been, and will continue to be, a primary driver for a large number of individuals and companies in deciding to hold membership in their industry organization.

Many non-profit organizations will define their knowledge management activities as keeping track of, and making easily available, their industry or professional knowledge and resources. They typically gather, catalog, and manage industry knowledge in the following typical areas:

- Policies, standards, and guidelines
- Best practices
- Trade press/scholarly journal articles
- News releases
- Other industry/profession specific documents
- Expert opinion
- Availability of, and access to, subject matter experts
- Peer review committees
- Research
- Surveys
- Safety and occupational issues
- Knowledge sources created by staff
- Collective industry/profession stakeholder knowledge

Chances are that a large segment of your members are not aware of the knowledge resources you make available to them. This can be a sad situation because so much of the potential ROI perceived by your members can be demonstrated in this feature of membership. It is very exciting to association executives when they realize that this is an amazing opportunity to accelerate member awareness of the value their organization delivers. Unfortunately, if you give away this knowledge to your industry at-large, you are encouraging people in the industry to say that membership is optional. This is "not" a good message. When executed properly, your knowledge management efforts should be a compelling reason for non-members to join.

As you learned in Chapter 4, the true real-dollar member-perceived value from each of your organization's features of membership—like this knowledge management example—can be calculated based upon:

- Total sum of industry knowledge available to members
- Member awareness that usable knowledge is available to them 24/7
- Timeliness, uniqueness, and distribution of proprietary knowledge
- Ease and speed of access to specific knowledge desires at any given time
- Resource acquisition time saving, measured in employee time and costs

While many of the above elements of member-value calculation might at first glance appear to be nebulous, they indeed can be measured. Proprietary knowledge availability and access, as a feature of membership, can be determined in real-dollars. This can be done by determining the actual cost of acquisition non-members might have to pay to access the same knowledge through alternative sources. Additionally, there is the real lost opportunity cost and/or negligence cost to the non-member's organization of not having timely access to the knowledge. While public knowledge management systems like Google do afford subscription-less access, the length of time that it might take to conduct the search, read through the numerous listings, and aggregate the needed knowledge—could be daunting, very time-consuming, and employee-cost expensive.

Chances are that a large segment of your members are not aware of the knowledge resources you make available to them

Unintended ROI Killer

If non-member, industry stakeholders, can access anything more than "industry headlines" through your website or from headquarters staff—what would urge them to invest their resources in membership? It is currently trendy for consultants to push the concept of *"Content Marketing"* as an up-to-date marketing effort in a highly engaged social media age. However, what they do not reveal is that this idea also kills the member-only benefit, thereby reducing *The ROI of Membership.* If your organization gives too much away under the guise of drawing people to the organization, the true result might very well be the opposite of your expectations—giving non-members yet another reason not to join.

Your organization must put a high value on your knowledge management activities, reserving all but the most basic "industry headlines" for members to access through password protected, members-only sections of your website. Headquarters staff must also be instructed in the fine art of only giving away a "taste" of knowledge—not the whole meal.

While it is frequently championed from association and society leaders, the worn out justification of giving knowledge away so that the non-members "MIGHT" see the value of membership and join is pure folly and delusion. If they have not joined by now, they're never going to join. These non-members are going to continue to bleed you dry, enjoying industry stakeholder benefit if you allow them to do so.

This idea extends into all the areas your organization offers features of membership, including member communities. Getting members communicating with one other is an excellent way to strengthen engagement and ROI. There are several types of physical and virtual member communities that can be encouraged, with noticeable advantages to each.

Your organization must put a high value on your knowledge management activities

Communities of Reciprocity—an Important Feature of Membership

Call them communities of practice, networks, special interest groups, mastermind groups, or communities of reciprocity—when your members are actively engaged in your organizations groups—there are two important benefits to the organization. First is what usually comes to mind—member retention. The second might not be at the top of one's mind and that is member recruitment. When a member is enthusiastically engaged, he or she will aggressively talk about the organization to colleagues, suppliers and customers. There is no better source for member recruitment, which will have the follow-up member assimilation factor included, than your ***Member Recruitment Evangelists***.

There is no better source for member recruitment, which will have the follow-up member assimilation factor included, than your Member Recruitment Evangelists

Like knowledge management, communities of reciprocity are a frequently overlooked in determining *The ROI of Membership*. These communities, which might be local, regional or virtual forums or casual gatherings, easily create and deliver multi-directional value. In many ways members are co-creating their own value proposition. Some members find a needed platform for their ideas, while others are more passive. Even with minimal participation, some members gain value simply from observing. This is especially common on the social media platforms.

High-level member engagement should be encouraged within communities of reciprocity. This is an important member ROI activity. However, there can be internal control issues applied to non-organization created communities that can easily squelch this kind of valuable participation.

This is a two-sided sword for association leadership and staff. While participant value is being created, if a particular community of reciprocity is not operating as an association sanctioned entity, then the leadership might consider the community a threat, menace, or danger to the organization's traditional power structure. This is truly a disappointment to mature organizational value seekers. Conversely, if the community is open to non-members, there is no member-only ROI and the value being created can erode the organization's total membership value proposition. This is where collaboration can offer the winning formula. Smart association executives are getting out in front of these communities and gently pulling them under the organization's umbrella, thereby adding another feature of membership to the total offering.

Member Created and Administered Communities

Awesome are the organizational communities of reciprocity that are member founded and supported by the organization from the start. While these communities might be erroneously feared by the ensconced organizational leadership, they are nevertheless conduits of high member value. Dynamic individuals drive the creation of communities that they want, need, and desire and the association should be right there to offer support.

If a contingency of your members want a particular community and develop it, they will value it and remain engaged as long as the community delivers value to them. It would only be a low-esteem, paranoid personality that would want to squelch this kind of community participation. Association leadership really should embrace these emerging communities or they risk repercussions of member anger and organizational abandonment.

This kind of dissatisfaction has been clearly experienced by the doctor members of the American Medical Association. An August 2011 article in the *Canadian Medical Association Journal* details the atrophy. It reveals that in the early 1950s, about 75% of US physicians were AMA members but in 2011 that number had dropped to approximately 15%. During the same time the state and specialty medical organizations have experienced remarkable growth. The doctors moved to segmented specialty associations and societies that were better meeting their needs.

Since these member-generated communities deliver additional organizational value to members, association and society leaders should be looking to put in place strategies and tactics that foster these communities rather than limiting them. Your member engagement department should be out in the marketplace scanning need and fostering these tight-knit local or geographically large social media groups. Frequently, geographical communities can evolve into a formal "chapter" structure far quicker and more successfully than can organization-developed units. This is because the organization might mistakenly be focused on revenue while the members are surely focused on personal value.

There is the need though for the organization to have a modicum of influence, especially if the group is using the organization's name or logo. This can be especially tricky if the members are allowed to run free and state anything they like on social media platforms. Care must be taken to avoid inviting litigation from slighted or disgruntled participants.

What's the answer? A partnership model can deliver both the value participants need while still affording the umbrella organization some assurances of proper participant behavior. If the group participants have a headquarters office or regional liaison that understands the value of collaboration over domination, the chances of a smooth operating and successful community of reciprocity are high.

Organization-Generated Communities

Control is one of the primary reasons that organizational leadership will squelch member-generated communities in favor of official organization-created communities. Organization-created communities are fine and can deliver high levels of value if created primarily to deliver additional value to members. If revenue generation is the primary organizational driver, newly created member communities have a higher propensity for failure.

Organization-created communities should serve the needs of members rather than an unstated agenda of the organization staff, or board member. There also is the important challenge of building relevant communities. Since member-created communities emanate from member needs, organization-created communities must do the same. In order to anticipate member desires, much more research than a simple survey is necessary. The challenge with surveying members using free or inexpensive online systems that do not offer a host of dynamic questioning methodologies is that the answers will be flawed.

It is not uncommon for a few members to state, "Give me this or that." Then the board jumps on it. However, when created by the organization, the members do not participate. Why? They cannot tell. It could be because of poor board decisions in direction or format, poor development or poor implementation. When members have "skin in the game" they are more apt to participate and perform. This is where the "SPIE" action model (scan, plan, implement and evaluate) will serve the organization well— get involvement not just cold survey information.

A better approach might be to employ a number of surveying and listening methods. Having staff listen to and record off-handed remarks made by members during a variety of events can be very valuable. When enough members have made similar remarks about a needed community— build it by involving those who have participated in creating the vision of what the community can be. This method is much more effective than going out and building communities without a champion.

Member Recruitment Evangelists make excellent champions of organization-created communities, member-created communities and most other variants. The champion operates a bit like the group leader, but without any formal title. The champion generally has a minimal personal agenda—if any—and rarely over exerts his/her position or perceived authority. The champion role is a very useful model for communities of reciprocity. The most important activity for an effective champion is that of cheerleader, motivator, and driver. Someone has to push to keep the community going.

When members have "skin in the game" they are more apt to participate and perform

Organization-Assisted Communities

A hybrid approach will generally serve most organizations and their members well. This is where member-generated communities of reciprocity are encouraged and assisted through a flexible support system put in place by the board of directors and administrated by the organization's staff.

When leaders, volunteer or paid, embrace communities of reciprocity that sprout within and around the organization, success is far more likely. These communities should not be feared but rather embraced, nourished, and encouraged. The natural byproduct is additional perceived value your members will experience from membership in your organization, additional reasons to be engaged, and the organic development of ***Member Recruitment Evangelists*** who will sing the praises of your organization. Work closely with all involved to help these types of member-only communities thrive. The result will be to dramatically increase the yearly sustainable real-dollar *ROI of Membership* for everyone.

Keep the value fresh in their heads and they will remember when it is time to renew

Put a Price on Everything

Pricing everything will dramatically increase your members' perception of their ROI. Anything that you make available to members should exhibit an honest "retail" price—everything from electronic newsletters to member lists to legislative updates—everything. To legitimize the price, offer those products, services, and access to non-members at the stated retail price. Don't think outsiders will pay? It doesn't matter. The point is for non-members to see what they could be getting for free or at a reduced price if they held membership and for members to see the value they are receiving. Do not make the mistake of letting members think it's free and possibly valueless. Help them to see the value and ROI.

Do your members call the headquarter office for advice when they get into a jam? Send them an invoice, zeroed out with an equal discount, just like any other professional service provider would do. This goes for other services the association provides "free of charge" for its members. Add a personal note, "So glad you felt comfortable calling and allowing us to serve." Every single day of the week you can warmly remind your members of the real-dollar value they receive because of their membership in your organization.

Keep the value fresh in their heads and they will remember when it is time to renew.

What Else Do You Have to Sell?

There is gold hidden in your organization's dusty shelves and forgotten computer files. Look around your organization for items, services, and various methods of access that might be perceived by non-members as highly valuable. Put a retail price on those items and services. Make them available to non-members at the retail price and to members at no charge or a greatly discounted price. The differential will add to your members' perception of their yearly membership ROI.

The rub here might be that some of your board members still hold on to their antiquated belief that all of the above is sacred and proprietary information and thereby not to be disseminated. Come on, it's the twenty-first century, let's move on and provide as much ROI for your members as possible!

You ask your members to make a payment each year. Each year when they make that payment to your organization they have to make a new decision to buy. Make it easy for your members to see that it is a good business decision to hold membership in your organization. Do this through higher ROI delivery and perception and guess what? They will become membership evangelists for your organization and convince their colleagues, many that you might never reach, to also join and partake of the plentiful ROI.

Every single day of the week you can warmly remind your members of the real-dollar value they receive because of their membership in your organization

In the table below are the actual features valuations of the various features of membership at a southeastern state specialty contractors association. While none of the features were valued in high numbers, there were a number of features that offered value. The high number of features valued at zero could be possible member-only value. However, several features were valued at zero because they were not member-only, members found no value in the feature, or because the pricing of the feature was no better than what was readily available from the private sector. An important discussion for your leadership might be around the question, which is more important to the organization, commissions or better pricing to the members. Check your organization to see how much of the potentially member-only value you are giving away to non-members of keeping for the organization itself. Put a fair price on everything.

$750	Networking	$300	Uniform Arbitration Program
$250	Business Insurance	$250	Business referrals from state organization web-site
$200	MSDS: Emergency roadside assistance	$200	Prescription Discount Card
$200	FleetBoss GPS	$200	Local Chapter Partici-pation
$200	Regulations Updates	$100	Design Awards
$100	Continuing Education Hours	$100	Using organization logo for building credibility
$100	Scholarships	$75	Organization provided collateral material
$50	Acxiom background check tool	$0	Health Insurance
$0	Quickbooks; Order programs, updates and training	$0	MSDS: Material Safety Data Sheets
$0	GreenFlag Profit Re-covery Services	$0	Constant Contact Email Marketing
$0	Mentoring	$0	Workers' Comp
$0	Employee Benefits Programs	$0	Credit card processing
$0	Holiday Cards	$0	Member Cruises
$0	Monthly Printed News-letter	$0	Weekly Electronic Newsletter
$0	Immediate Legislative Updates		

Figure 6

Specific Features of Membership

The following listed features of membership have been separated into four basic categories. The annual real-dollar value (total divided average) that associations deliver to members in each category is:

- $3,944 for Professional Development
- $7,153 for Business Solutions
- $2,430 for Knowledge Management

- $2,764 for Networking

These averages and those listed below were derived from an amalgamation of approximately 50 qualitative research valuation sessions conducted from 2001 through 2012. These included trade associations and professional societies, both individual and company member organizations, and membership numbers ranging from 300 to 100,000. Since this is a collection, not all organizations offered all features. As such, it is recommended not to publish these below-listed numbers for your members but rather to use them as a guide for discussion. The one exception was the separate valuations for supplier members which, as you would expect, always hiked networking and various other line-item numbers based on their increased business development interest and opportunities.

> ***Note:*** *Total organizational ROI value numbers were not included because of the differential between individual and company memberships. In a number of cases, when it was the company that belonged to the membership organization, the real-dollar value numbers listed below would need to be multiplied by the number of employees, executives or users within the company. If your organization has company memberships, then for several of the below listed line-items, you will need to multiply by the average number of employees to get the true real-dollar benefit number. Also, in very rare situations when an item was evaluated by only one organization, that line-item was not included in the below list.*

You will notice below that there are two numbers for each feature of membership. The first, larger number was calculated by only adding and averaging organizations where their members determined the feature to be member-only. The second, smaller number was calculated by dividing the total number of organizations Rigsbee Research measured by the total value, even when the value was zero because of not being a member-only feature. This gives an indication that in some cases; too many organizations are giving away too much value.

When the numbers are close, that means that the feature was most likely valuated as member-only in the majority of sessions. If your organization delivers a below-listed feature as member-only, the first, larger number should be used when comparing your total value proposition. While you could use the below numbers to build a member recruitment brochure—stating "association averages," it is far better to do your own qualitative research focus group sessions to be able to state, "Our members say this is the average real-dollar value they receive."

Professional Development ROI Numbers

- $3,300/$953 for income differential enabled through Industry Certifications
- $1,240/$799 for the gained Knowledge and Education afforded through the Opportunity to Participate in Leadership Positions
- $1,189/$238 for Travel Cost Tax Savings from Conference and Other Meeting Attendance
- $1,020/$634 for Peer Support and Mentoring (receiving and giving)
- $981/$371 for Component, Constituent, Chapter and Special Interest Group Access
- $897/$159 for Access to National Organization's Meetings and various other Resources

- $807/$238 for Job Leads
- $634/$226 for Career Development Opportunities and Services
- $625/$278 for Peer and Industry Prestige, Recognition and Awards
- $555/$160 for Certification Study Groups and Local Testing

Business Solution ROI Numbers

- $3,814/$593 for Safety Programs, Education and Resources
- $3,673/$1,061 for Organization Enabled Business Development Opportunities and Peer Referrals
- $3,018/$1,006 for Affinity Program Savings on Actual Usage
- $2,169/$386 for the Cost Savings and Opportunity to Find New Suppliers and Service Providers
- $2,091/$790 for Innovative Business and Practice Solutions
- $1,692/$226 for Access to other Industry or Related Organizations through Organization's Affiliation and Membership
- $1,495/$1,395 for Training; Business, Technology, Marketing, Sales, Management, Leadership and Industry Specific Topics
- $1,060/$707 for Coupons and Discounts or Access to Organization's Goods and Services

- $1,021/$544 for Access to Headquarter and Field Office Executives and Staff
- $828/$294 for Credibility with Customers, Publicity and Image through Membership and Logo usage
- $650/$43 for Product Knowledge gained through meetings
- $560/$62 for Cost Savings in Finding New Employees
- $410/$46 for Legal Seminars and Consultations

Knowledge Management ROI Numbers

- $1,957/$783 for Industry Research, including Benchmarking and Compensation Studies
- $1,849/$740 for Legislative Updates
- $658/$278 for Member-Only Section on Organization's Web Site
- $587/$157 for Industry Standards and Codes.
- $542/$169 for Weekly and Monthly e-zine or e-news
- $308/$117 for Print and Electronic Journals and Resource Access
- $261/$110 for Member Directory and Directory Services
- $146/$78 for Printed Magazines and Newsletters

Networking ROI Numbers

- $2,763 for Networking (While there are many ways to look at networking, it was valuated based on business development and profit opportunities, cost and loss savings and many other considerations—and a catch-all for all other benefits not included in the above line-items.)

In reviewing the above, you can get a good idea of how association and society members across North America have valued specific member-only products and services or differentials between member and non-member prices in annual real-dollar benefit numbers. If you are giving away any of the listed features, you can quickly determine how much member-only value is slipping away and you will have a better idea on how to shore up *The ROI of Membership* in your organization.

Leaders in association management have been preaching this gospel for quite some time

What to Keep & What to Dump

It is crucial for any membership organization's leadership to understand which features of membership are most relevant to the majority of members. Leaders in association management have been preaching this gospel for quite some time—at least since the beginning of the twenty-first century and earlier. Michael Olson, when he was president and CEO at the American Society of Association Executives was quoted in the September 16, 2002 issue of *Meeting-News*, answering the question about the single biggest challenge that associations face at that time. His response, *"It's focusing effectively on their most relevant programs—walking away from peripherally valuable programs and not offering the same level of benefits and services they have historically. It's a good time for associations to rethink what they're doing for their members and what their members value most."*

The following year, ASAE's new president and CEO, John Graham IV, was asked the similar question by *Association News* in their August 2003 issue. *"What do you consider to be the major issue facing the association management profession in 2003?* His answer, *"Clearly, translating the mission of the organization and the needs and wants of the members, and being able to sustain that model economically is a balancing act. So many associations are chasing after dollars and revenue streams that may or may not be in alignment with the overall mission of the organization."*

Add to the idea, Twentieth Century management guru, Peter Drucker wisely observed, *"The essence of strategy is denial."* If you don't say "no" to the things that aren't worth doing, you will never have the energy, time and resources to do what matters to your members. You don't have to do everything; it is wise to do the right things very well.

If you are giving away any of the listed features, you can quickly determine how much member-only value is slipping away

How to Conduct the Features of Membership Value Discovery Exercise

Have your board of directors and your headquarters staff members complete a *Member Value/Resource Allocation Framework Process*—together or separately. This will help everyone get a better idea of which of your organization's features of membership are member-perceived, high value and low cost to the organization as opposed to which are low value and high cost to the organization.

This framework was developed by Rigsbee Research as an exercise for its Member ROI Summit™. It is very important for every organization to deliver the maximum number of highly valued features of membership in order to achieve explosive growth. If you are spending too much money in delivering a particular feature of membership that is also valued low by the majority of members, you will want to reconsider offering that feature.

This exercise will help your organization to better realize where resources might or might not be invested. Consider suspending high cost/low value features in favor of investing your resources in additional low cost/high value features that will increase *The ROI of* Membership as perceived by your members.

1. Plan a meeting at a time and place where there will be little chance of interruption. Gather the participants and give everyone the chart (figure 7) on the following page.

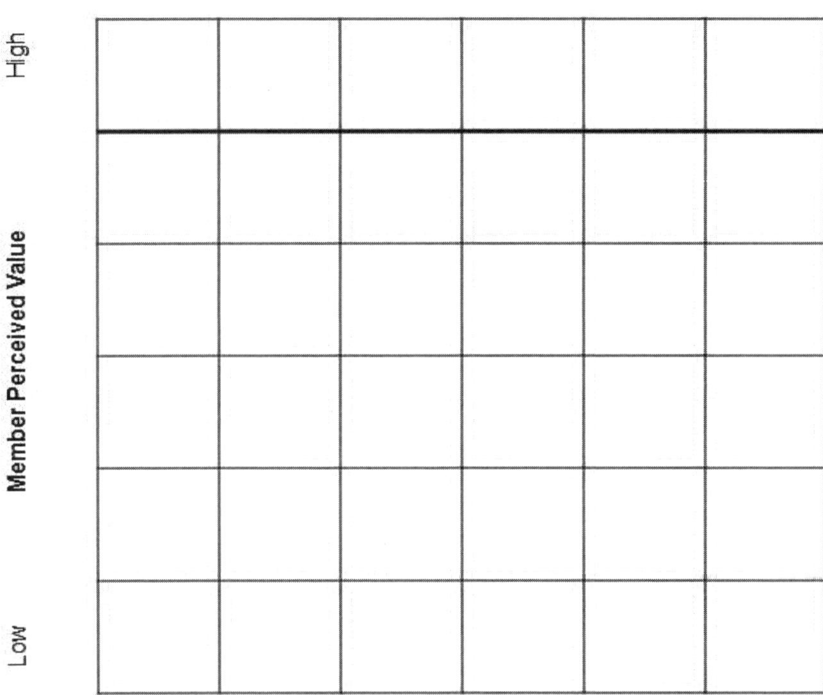

Figure 7

2. Have everyone list 10-20 of your organization's features of membership: both services and products.

3. Number the list and then plot each of the features, just the corresponding number, on the graph as in figure 8. Each person will determine from their own perspective. The vertical axis is for how one thinks the members perceive the value of each feature. The horizontal axis is for actual cost to the organization to produce or deliver the product or service. For features only considered valuable to a few, you will have to push that feature more toward the "high cost." You will notice that feature #2 is placed at a higher

cost than you otherwise might consider because of low member usage. For example you might, or might not, list some of the following:

1) Closed LinkedIn Member Community
2) Golf Tournament at Annual Meeting
3) Organization Published Books
4) Legislative Updates
5) Industry Awards

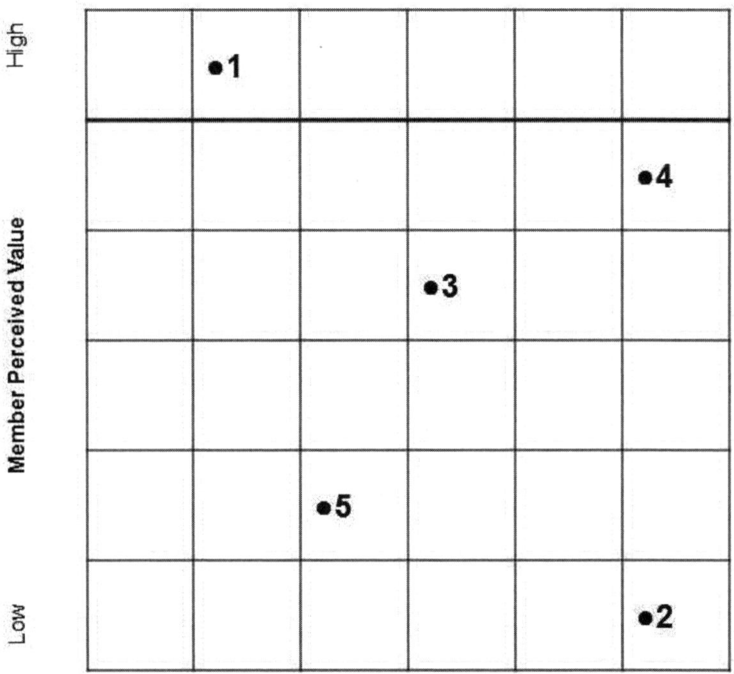

Figure 8

4. After everyone in the room, volunteer leaders and staff has completed the above directions, have them overlay the quadrant dividers on their work as illustrated in figure 9. Then explain why the top left is the

best quadrant and the bottom right is the worst based on cost-benefit analysis.

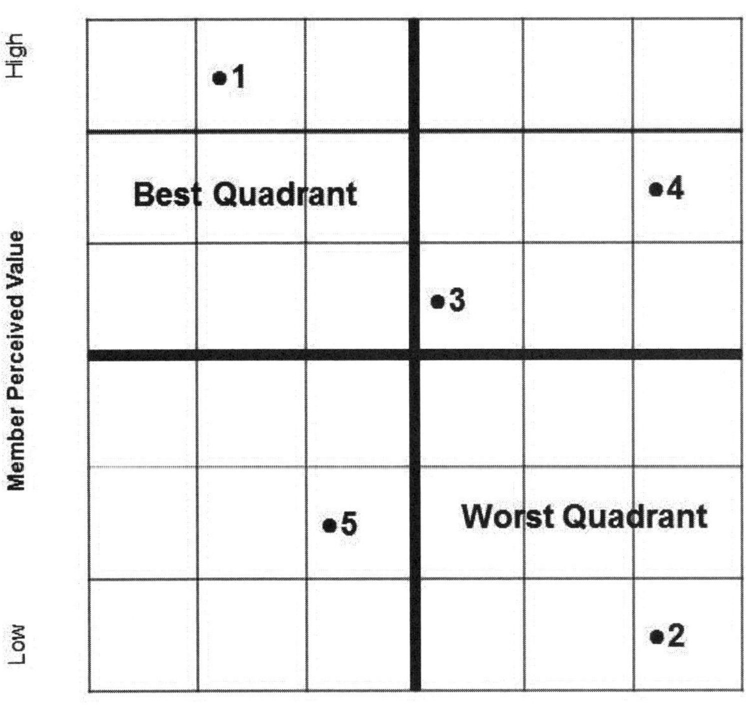

Figure 9

5. Armed with this information, everyone can enter into a substantive discussion about the future viability of the various features of membership based on the cost/value analysis. This will be an eye-opening discussion for your organization's leaders.

Figure out for what reasons your members join—what differentiates your organization. Also, determine what members or prospective members are looking for in a first class organization. Then you can determine if your organization scores well in those areas. If the organization scores well in areas that the members are not looking for, they are less important and should be given less emphasis. Perhaps it's time to dump less important features—in favor of focusing on more important features of membership?

Chapter 5 Executive Action Steps

1. First, determine the potential member-only features that your organization is currently giving away and discontinue the practice. If there are products or services that you believe should be available to non-members, put a price on them. This way the differential between member and non-member price becomes a member-only benefit.

2. Second, to further ratchet up your total membership value proposition a few more notches, you will want to consider making some of your current member-only services and products available to non-members for a price. If you are giving products and services to your members at no charge, while that is awesome for the members, there will always be a perception challenge that your members will not appreciate the value. However, when listing on your website products and services at no or low charge to members and at a higher charge to non-members, your members instantly see one more factor contributing to *The ROI of Membership.*

3. Have a discussion with your legal counsel about non-member pricing. It is important to add a cautionary word about member and non-member pricing. If the differential on any single product, service, or conference is such that it compels membership, there is a good chance that you are leaving your organization in a vulnerable and possible indefensible position should antitrust litigation arise. Many non-profit organizations appear to be guilty of doing the above. However, as long as nobody ever launches litigation for the practice, said organizations can go along "fat, dumb, and happy." The goal is not to scare you but to inform you that there is federal law that prevents your organization from pricing that would force a person or organization to join. This book does not offer legal advice so it is important to have a discussion with your organization's legal

counsel if you feel you might have concern in this area.

4. Visit www.rigsbee.com/roi5.htm for a video chapter review and additional ideas from the author.

Chapter 6

Start Selling Value, Not Guilt

There are two opposing membership viewpoints in association management: the traditional perspective suggesting that people should support their industry or profession by joining—simply because they should—the "good of the order" argument. If you have gotten this far into the book, you realize this perspective most likely is not working for you or your organization.

The other perspective is that of recruiting members based on value. You recognize that value is in the eye of the beholder—value can be elusive for the uninitiated. While it is true that people do join a membership organization for a number of different reasons, in today's world the "what's in it for me" prevails over the "how can I serve." As we proceed in this chapter, it will be revealed how you and your organization can sell membership based on member-only features and their benefits, and you will learn how to do this through the window of buying motives.

Your industry stakeholders, the non-members, really would want to join your membership organization. Unfortunately, they don't realize it. They need an awakening, and it is your organization's responsibility to provide just that. Your organization's membership prospects must first understand the all-important, **what's in it for me**. As you draw these prospects closer to membership, they must see the possibility of real, honest, and measurable ROI for their time and money. You then can clearly answer their most pressing question: **What's in it for me?**

People do join a membership organization for a number of different reasons

Feature versus Benefit

Through extensive research of membership organizations' websites, one would likely discover that few understand member benefits. Benefits are the things that make members' lives better. The features of membership are the items available to members to utilize or ignore. As an example, access to an affinity program is a feature of membership. The member benefit of an affinity program is that it delivers more business, more money, cost savings, etc. to the member.

Be careful with affinity programs. If the member price/benefit ratio is not substantially greater as a "feature of membership" than otherwise might be available in the general marketplace, this feature offers no value. Your organization's decisions in the area of royalties or commissions received from the affinity program provider could very well eliminate the financial benefit to your members. You have to ask, "What is the highest good: dollars in the organization's bank account or valuable features of membership?" Generally there are rarely enough margins for affinity program companies to deliver both.

Even worse is when an organization espouses that its members should support their organization by participating in a particular affinity program that really is not a good financial decision for members. This is old paradigm thinking and inhibits member renewals. Review your current programs. Seek new products, services, and programs that deliver real-dollar value to members that is far beyond what non-member industry participants may enjoy. The **member-only benefit** is what will compel non-members to join.

Here's another example of benefits: Your organization is aggressive in advocacy and affecting legislation in your industry. Everyone gets the value regardless of holding membership in your organization. However, you might also send to your members a legislative update keeping them informed of your progress, results, and how recent legislation affects their business.

If you only send this out to members and, at the very most, only offer simple headlines via email blasts and website postings to non-members—you have an awesome feature of membership in the legislative update. Offering timely and accurate information about legislation and regulatory issues can save your members time, money, and heartache if they heed your warnings and information as it applies to their businesses. This feature of membership, the legislative update, delivers an important and highly valuable benefit through timely knowledge and awareness that one only receives through their membership.

Benefits are the things that make members' lives better

Feature of Membership Benefit Statements

In the previous chapter, you learned the average actual real-dollar value numbers for the various features of membership that were measured by an assortment of associations and societies. Since not every organization offers the same features, and not every member will use each feature available to them, it is crucial for a potential member's value perception to clearly understand how each feature will make their life better. The better your organization can communicate the actual *BENEFITS* that the member will receive, the higher the total value perception. Below, you will find the benefits (how it makes the member's life better) of many of those features.

Professional Development Benefit Copy

- **Component, Constituent, Chapter and Special Interest Group Access** *(Member Benefit: Having access to local communities of reciprocity helps a member feel more secure in their industry by knowing that, close at hand, there are colleagues who can help in areas ranging from personal to professional to organizational. There is also the time and cost savings of having colleagues close or being part of a specific interest community as opposed to the costs of traveling to national meetings or looking for specific help from the organization's general population.)*

- **Access to National Organization's Meetings and various other Resources** *(Member Benefit: Holding membership in a state, regional or local organization and having the access to a national or international organization, members can easily gain more industry knowledge quickly and to get a broader perspective compared to provincial. There is also frequently a time and cost savings in accessing resources, some that might not be easily accessible otherwise.)*

- **Career Development Opportunities and Services** *(Member Benefit: For the person who wants to improve their career and earning prospects, frequently, the resources, activities and mentoring that are available to them from their association or society are far beyond the scope of what might be available from their employer. Additionally, the anonymity can potentially* *help a person to keep their job, and income, while seeking out other opportunities.)*

- **Gained Knowledge and Education afforded through the Opportunity to Participate in Leadership Positions** *(Member Benefit: The value of this benefit is huge as one can learn and make mistakes in their role of volunteer leader while learning and not making the potentially very costly, money and position, mistakes within the context of employment or their own company. The additional education given by many associations and societies to their volunteer leaders is close in educational value to receiving an MBA, but without the astronomical price tag. The hands on experiential value can take years off of one's managerial learning curve.)*

- **Income differential enabled through Industry Certifications** *(Member Benefit: Certifications generally deliver more income to the holders than without. This could mean higher salary income, greater customer numbers, or higher revenue through enhanced service fees.)*

- **Certification Study Groups and Local** Testing *(Member Benefit: Time and travel expense savings is the most frequent benefit. Also, having the ability to interact with industry colleagues in gaining certification readiness training is frequently cited as a confidence booster and element in first attempt success.)*

- **Peer Support and Mentoring (receiving and giving)** *(Member Benefit: Benefit is received from both giving and receiving. Through offering mentoring one can fulfill the need for legacy and the pride/prestige buying motive of continued membership. On the receiving side, the benefit is generally a greatly reduced learning curve in one's industry or profession, saving the time and cost of needless beginner mistakes. For the employee, there is career acceleration. For the* *business owner there is revenue acceleration, cost reduction and better supplier and customer selection.)*

- **Peer and Industry Prestige, Recognition and Awards** *(Member Benefit: Prestige delivers benefit through a number of conduits such as the ease of entering collegial groups, opening doors among colleagues, customers and suppliers, securing premiere projects and customers, better employees, referrals, and many others.)*

- **Job Leads** *(Member Benefit: Depending on the industry or profession, job and customer leads through one's association or society can easily represent 25% of revenues, without the marketing effort and expense. For the individual, it can frequently mean an additional $10K to $30K in yearly income.)*

- **Travel Cost Tax Savings from Conference and Other Meeting Attendance** *(Member Benefit: Everybody loves it when Uncle Sam partially pays for an activity and this is very common for members of associations and societies. Attending an educational conference or buying show is a legitimate business expense, and tax deduction. For many organizations, vendors also sponsor the events, reducing even further, the real event cost.)*

Business Solution Benefit Copy

- **Affinity Program Savings on Actual Usage** *(Member Benefit: Generally this area offers simple dollar/cash discounts on frequently used products and services over what one might find in the open marketplace.)*

- **Training; Business, Technology, Marketing, Sales, Management, Leadership and Industry Specific Topics** *(Member Benefit: There are usually substantial cost and travel savings, along with an important convenience factor for organized training compared to* *knowledge gained in the open market. Additionally, some of the education might not be available anywhere else which puts members ahead of their nonmembers in cutting edge knowledge and skills that will generally result in more and better revenues and reduced costs and expenditures.)*

- **Safety Programs, Education and Resources** *(Member Benefit: Here, respondents frequently mentioned dramatically lower costs, per employee, for safety programs, reduced travel and paid employee time in the training, and better availability. The per employee savings, in many cases both time and cost savings, coupled with better availability, made this benefit worth the cost of membership.)*

- **Access to Headquarter and Field Office Executives and Staff** *(Member Benefit: There are two important benefits to consider here: one is the shear cost/time savings of getting questions answered by headquarter staff and the second benefit is the availability of hard to find information. Frequently, a call to the association/society's headquarter office could save members several hours and, more times than not, several dollars...into the thousands. Having a daily live personal resource available can also eliminate costly mistakes and potential fines. This is one of the most under-realized benefits of membership.)*

- **Innovative Business and Practice Solutions** *(Member Benefit: Sometimes the answers come from association headquarter staff, sometimes from colleagues, and sometimes from conference programming. However, numerous responses cited several thousands of dollars in cost savings and lost time that was not squandered needlessly based on innovations and solutions learned through associations and societies.)*

- **Cost Savings and Opportunity to Find New Suppliers and Service Providers** *(Member Benefit: Many* *a business owner can spin tales of suppliers from Hell. The benefits of selecting the right supplier include consistency of supply and billing, the costs form selecting the wrong suppler can include production stoppage, diminished quality and billing errors. Selecting the right supplier saves time and money, while increasing productivity and quality.)*

- **Cost Savings in Finding New Employees** *(Member Benefit: There is always a hard cost associated with acquiring new employees; search cost and training cost. Discounts or even access to industry job posting sites can be meaningful. Finding better employees through an association's job posting service can save an organization time and money while attracting more qualified candidates and offering a modicum of assurance as to the quality of the new employee.)*

- **Legal Seminars and Consultations** *(Member Benefit: The benefit of legal seminars is avoiding the pain of litigation through cutting-edge and industry-specific legal knowledge and learning to understand its application. Additionally, the benefit of complementary legal consultations includes both cost savings and the comfort that comes from working with lawyers who have industry specific knowledge and experience.)*

- **Product Knowledge Gained Through Meetings** *(Member Benefit: While it is fair to state that non-members can also gain the above knowledge by attending meetings, members generally receive discounts delivering a cost-savings benefit. Members tend to be better informed about meetings and through regular participation, build information-revealing relationships. The additional benefit is saving time gathering industry knowledge at one location where suppliers are readily available to reveal intensively descriptive product information.)*

- **Credibility with Customers, Publicity and Image through Membership and Logo Usage** *(Member Benefit: Affiliation and alignment with a recognized non-profit organization delivers higher credibility in the minds of many customers and suppliers. This credibility leads to more business with better quality customers and relationships with quality suppliers. The result of this is almost always better profitability for the individual or company member.)*

- **Access to other Industry or Related Organizations through Organization's Affiliation and Membership** *(Member Benefit: This access can deliver cost savings through not having to hold dual memberships. Also, by participating in an organization that the member might not otherwise be aware of offers expanded networking, knowledge, and access possibilities.)*

- ***Coupons and Discounts or Access to Organization's Goods and Services*** *(Member Benefit: Members realize cost savings and have an increased likelihood of using an organization's unique products or services that might not otherwise have been accessible.)*

- **Organization Enabled Business Development Opportunities and Peer Referrals** *(Member Benefit: More business is available to members through additional channels and access to new market segments.)*

Knowledge Management Benefit Copy

- **Weekly and Monthly e-zine or e-news** *(Member Benefit: Timely information, depending on the industry or profession, can be hugely valuable in many ways. This benefit can minimize the chances for loss through regulatory fines and realize gains through an increased awareness of emerging opportunities. There is also a time savings by having information spoon-fed,* *rather than having to spend time and resources acquiring this information through internal staff.)*

- **Printed Magazines and Newsletters** *(Member Benefit: Similar to above.)*

- **Legislative Updates** *(Member Benefit: This is somewhat similar in value to print and electronic newsletters and magazines but with a big difference in the area of time savings. Time savings truly equate to dollar savings and bottom-line profitability.)*

- **Member-Only Section on Organization's Website** *(Member Benefit: If your organization has most of its premium and crucial industry information locked behind a password protected member-only section of your website giving nothing more than basic headlines to non-members, the content is highly valuable to members. While you do compete against Google in the area of knowledge management; specific information might be hard to find through search engines. Also, the speed with which your members can access exactly what they need delivers a cost saving benefit.)*

- **Industry Standards and Codes** *(Member Benefit: Providing members with access to this information can save them the cost of expensive volumes, code, and regulatory books.)*

- **Member Directory and Directory Services** *(Member Benefit: This is particularly valuable to vendor/supplier members for prospecting new business. All the industry contact information in one document is also a time saver and business development opportunity. For non-vendor members— having easy access to members is quite convenient and saves time when contacting colleagues.)*

- **Industry Research, including Benchmarking and Compensation Studies** *(Member Benefit: This is in-*

formation that is frequently not available to non-members, even for a premium price. It can be helpful in providing valuable information for a company's strategic decisions in moving forward and frequently reveals competitive industry and opportunity trends. These tools, if used correctly, can give members a competitive edge over non-members.)

- **Print and Electronic Journals and Resource Access** *(Member Benefit: There is typically a common member discounted price and a non-member retail price that delivers cost savings on industry specific data. Also, there is an advantage for members because associations generally publicize the release of this kind of data to members long before the industry in general, offering a competitive advantage to members.)*

Networking Benefit Copy

- **Networking** (*Member Benefit: While there are many ways to look at networking, the way this feature makes a member's life better is based on increased business development opportunities that generate increased profit opportunities, cost and loss savings through learning new techniques, and not falling prey to the wrong suppliers.*

- **Other** *(There are many other random benefits and value that might not be included in the above features and benefits list.*)

Time savings truly equate to dollar savings and bottom-line profitability

Buying Motives

As stated above, the legislative update is a feature of membership that delivers a clear benefit to the member. The benefit of this feature is how the update makes the lives of your members better. This benefit, perhaps, would most likely satisfy the buying motive of *profit and gain*, as well as that of *fear of loss*, and possibly *avoidance of pain*. When you describe "how it makes their life better" benefit through the windows of buying motives, you will have created persuasively powerful marketing and sales copy.

The *Six Buying Motives* from Homer Smith, editor of *Master Salesmanship*, a print newsletter, published by Clement Communications from 1981-2003. Having had a number of discussions on this topic with Smith where he shared his insights. What you will read below are the translations and adaptations for the membership organization market. When you understand how to write *benefit sales copy* to sell your features of membership through all the various *buying motives*, your member recruitment marketing and sales efforts will become unstoppable.

1. Profit and Gain
2. Fear of Loss
3. Avoidance of Pain
4. Comfort and Pleasure
5. Love and Affection
6. Pride and Prestige

The buying motives are crucially important for every association executive, director of membership, and key volunteer leaders to clearly understand and embrace in both word and deed. These should be kept at top-of-mind when developing any member recruitment marketing materials.

Profit and Gain Buying Motive

This motive is especially strong for vendor/supplier members. Membership for business acceleration and increase is frequently the motivation for many business or professional persons to join their trade association or professional society. They do so with the hope of securing ideas and finding help in business and career improvement. Their perspective of membership is "Show me the money!"

Your members will need and want to learn. You will need to ensure that your programming is innovative and offers industry-specific, business growth and career/personal growth education. Raising caution flag for you—remember that *free* programming and education from suppliers and consultants can sometimes be worth only what it costs. Innovation and new answers will often come from outside the industry. This is where organizations must look to offer true value to their members rather than be tightfisted with their time and financial resources.

Fear of Loss Buying Motive

Continuing with the legislative example, your members (depending on the industry) might constantly be operating in fear of failure to follow (ever changing) regulatory policy and procedure. This fear of lost time, temporary shut-down or even permanent closure can weigh heavily on your members. Your legislative update can help members have the peace of mind that their association is watching out for them on a daily basis. For members of professional societies, this buying motive may emanate from concern of losing credentials or licenses. Others might fear losing their job if they are not able to keep up to date within their industry or specialty area.

Avoidance of Pain Buying Motive

Receiving crucial legislative and regulatory update information in a timely manner can very well save a business from potential fines and penalties from unexpected government agency visits. Any business owner or executive would gladly embrace methods for avoiding the pain of regulatory fines or temporary shut-downs.

When association executives speak with potential members, the default position frequently is to talk about providing legislative updates for members but to forget to translate the value of the updates for the potential member based on the person's personal or organizational buying motives.

Special Note: *The remaining three buying motives are a bit softer in perceived value, nevertheless are important to understand as stakeholders will also make their buying decision based on them.*

Comfort and Pleasure Buying Motive

The famous WalMart founder, Sam Walton, for years worked at a plywood desk—a sheet of plywood resting on two sawhorses, in the upstairs stockroom of one of his early stores. What kind of a desk do you work at? What kind of an office do you have? My guess is that your work environment is a bit more luxurious than that of Walton's. Do you really need it? Who knows—but what we do know is that you were motivated by the buying motive of comfort and pleasure to have the work environment that you currently enjoy.

What about your members? Does your membership organization offer its members the comfort and pleasure of knowing that they will be kept up to date on the industry's best practices, rules/regulations, and industry news? This saves a member time, mental space and stress, and the need for constant industry scanning since your association regularly does this for its members.

Membership for affiliation tends to fall into the comfort and pleasure motive. While perhaps somewhat less tangible, many simply have the desire to participate and assist in their industry or profession. This was a primary motivator for the Baby Boomers and those that came before. However, today's emerging leaders are focusing less on that motive and more on some sort of a return on their time and money investment—the (profit and gain motive). For many younger leaders of today, affiliation in itself is no longer reason enough.

Love and Affection Buying Motive

Believe it or not, even business leaders and owners need collegiality. This is one of the great benefits associations and societies offer to their members the bringing together of industry members through meetings and other methods. People need recognition; I conducted an extensive study on this topic throughout the United States in the mid-1990s. Many industry leaders truly need the adulation of their industry colleagues and associations can provide this through leadership opportunities, awards, and credential programs. They join their industry associations and societies to get what they perhaps do not get on the job—a little love and appreciation.

Pride and Prestige Buying Motive

Some associations and societies have done a fabulous job of creating the perception within their industry that it is prestigious to belong to the organization. With this prestige, comes the pride of membership and belonging. Consider the Los Angeles County Bar Association's Dinosaur Program. This is a special added membership, only available to LACBA paid members. It is for senior lawyers in their 60s and older—the association provides special programming just for them. They even get a LACBA lapel pin that is a little different, with a dinosaur in the center. The Dinosaur members are very proud to wear their distinguished lapel pin. With the right spin and group, even an extinct dinosaur can be used as a symbol of value for the right kind of prestige.

Organizations that offer valuable credentialing tend to serve members in the area of profit/gain and pride/prestige. The idea of value in certification and credentialing is important to explore. While many organizational certifications serve the members' desire for prestige, the American Society for Quality offers a credential to its members—one that actually translates into an additional yearly income of approximately $5,000 for the members who hold the credential.

Beware, though, as many organizations offer credentials but invest no money in the promotion of the credentials to the members' marketplace, thereby diminishing the value and sometimes only delivering value to the person that holds the credential. For the motive, profit/gain or pride/prestige, perceived value is the key. Just developing credentialing and certification programs without investing in the market promotion rarely offers actual real-dollar value to members.

When you understand how to write benefit sales copy to sell your features of membership through all the various buying motives, your member recruitment marketing and sales efforts will become unstoppable

Sell to the Primary Buying Motive

Association executives would do well to take the time to ask more questions about what a potential member is looking to receive through membership in their organization. Focus on explaining the benefits they will receive from the features of membership. Do this through the window of the prospect's primary, and perhaps secondary, buying motive. Your sales (membership) marketing materials and presentation should prove to be quite successful.

Many of the key features of membership that your organization offers speak directly to potential member buying motives. Don't try to sell what you are already giving away for free. Ultimately, they want to know what's in it for them in the areas of career, community, knowledge, solutions, and access. Focus on the areas of value where they can only receive the benefits through holding membership.

This chapter has provided an exhaustive buying motive list. The goal is not to list everything— until a prospect's eyes glaze over. Better is to use your knowledge of an individual or a particular sub-group's buying motives to select those member-only benefits that will get them to stand up and pay attention. You want to turn those prospects' eyes from a glaze to a glow.

Many of the key features of membership that your organization offers speak directly to potential member buying motives

Value Triangle

Twentieth Century conventional business wisdom was that everyone's value proposition was based on *price, quality* and *service* triangle—customers could pick any two. See figure 10. If one wanted higher quality and/or service, one would have to pay a higher price. If one wanted to pay a lower price, one would have to give up some quality and/or service. Seems reasonable enough—right?

While this idea still holds some truth today, Internet capabilities have released the access and price lock that retailers, distributors, and particularly membership organizations had enjoyed. Today, your members are empowered in their *consumer role* and are demanding all three—they want price, quality and service. If they cannot get what they want at brick and mortar outlets, they will turn to online shopping. These same people in their *member role* are now demanding the same in all areas of life. If the membership organization cannot deliver, they will move on. In many ways, your membership organization competes with Google daily, particularly in the area of knowledge management, on a daily basis. Are you ready? If not, get ready if you want to survive as an association.

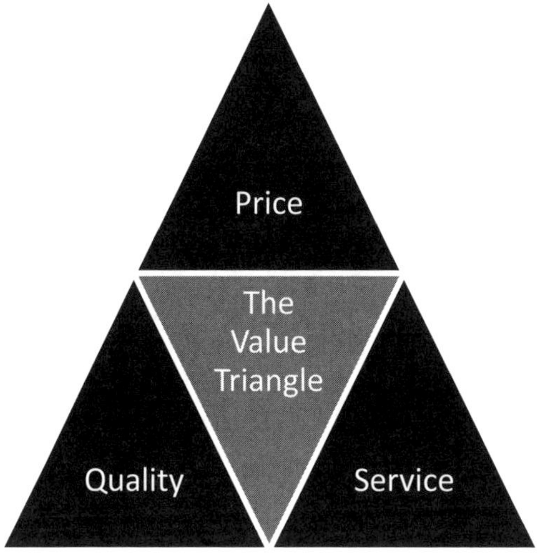

Figure 10

Author's Personal Story

Sell to your market. Recently, a state professional society gave me their Annual Report/Member Recruitment DVD. It was part of the materials for preparation of my qualitative research session with the society. While it was very nicely done and very professional, it totally missed the mark. During my research session with the group I asked for whom the DVD was intended. The board members in the room looked a bit perplexed and really did not have an answer. I then asked my question through a different perspective. I asked within your profession, which market segment would be their best likelihood of recruiting new members. They all stated, "The ones fresh out of school."

I went on to explain to those in attendance that the DVD was basically Baby Boomer members speaking to potential Baby Boomer members. The DVD mostly touted the opportunities to be involved in the organization's philanthropic work and the organization's prowess in affecting legislation in the statehouse. The DVD was pretty much an essay on Boomer members moving from being highly successful in their practices to being significant in their lives. It was a great Baby Boomer marketing piece.

The problem was that the Boomers were the wrong market segment. They wanted to recruit younger members with this DVD.

That's where the largest new member potential could be found. Let's face the facts, I told them. The new professionals are both trying to build a practice and simultaneously attempting to pay off their college loans. While they might care about becoming significant, what's really on their mind is building their practice. They are not even successful yet, let alone thinking of being significant. The DVD, as a Generation Y marketing tool, was effectively worthless.

The medium is also crucial. How do potential members want to consume information? After telling the above story at a recent Member ROI Summit™, one of the younger attendees, a director of membership, scoffed at the idea of producing a DVD. She said, "Why produce a DVD at all? My generation would prefer to watch on YouTube or download from the iTunes Store." Wow, she was right! There you have it—directly from the mouths of the generation your organization must influence in order to succeed.

The important take-away learning point for you here is to know to whom you are marketing and attempting to sell. Know their pain and their buying motives. If this means that you must segment your marketing materials, so be it. But whatever you do, do not make the mistake of attempting to sell irrelevant member-only or industry stakeholder benefits. Let your organization be the solution to their pain—communicate the solution well, and non-members will become members.

Let your organization be the solution to their pain

Too often, people only change when confronted with strong leadership, crisis, or both. Therefore, unless your members are willing to be at the whim of crises, strong leadership armed with the right information—from which your association can provide—is the only reliable change force they have. Fear of loss is a powerful and necessary buying motive. Take advantage of it.

Chapter 6 Executive Action Steps

1. With an understanding of the chapter concepts, improve the member-perceived value of each feature of membership your organization offers. Go through the list that is on your website. To develop excellent sales-copy for your website and promotional marketing materials, translate each feature into benefit that it delivers. Next, determine which buying motive(s) would most likely apply. Now re-write your copy explaining the benefit delivered through the buying motive window. This is the kind of benefit description that few membership organizations are able to create.

2. Produce worksheets like figure 11. List your organization's key features of membership; products, services, etc. Complete the worksheet yourself and have various department leaders (membership, communications, marketing, HR, financial, etc.) independently also do the same. Overlay everyone's answers for a more complete and multi-faceted perspective. You will now be able to effectively communicate to your market the, "What's in it for me?"

Feature of Membership	Likely Buying Motive	Benefit (How it makes their life better)

Figure 11

3. Visit www.rigsbee.com/roi6.htm for a video chapter review and additional thoughts from the author

Chapter 7

Membership is Everybody's Business

Are you ready for explosive member recruitment to go viral? Do you want passion for your member ROI to be contagious? Help is on the way. This final chapter is really about helping you to convert your members into ***Member Recruitment Evangelists***. You'll need to arm them with the proper tools so they can effortlessly and successfully spread the good news about your organization throughout your industry. A crucial tool as you are aware by now is the knowledge of *The ROI of Membership* that your organization delivers. In short, it will help your organization prove to the industry that membership is a smart career, business, and financial decision.

Everything shared with you thus far has feed and supported the ideas that will follow. Membership really is everybody's business. Your method for selling and marketing to potential members will likely be determined by many factors, some out of your control, but most easily within your control. Never let what you can't control stop you from doing what you can and must do, to help your organization reach its full member recruitment potential.

Three Recruitment Methods

There are three basic member recruitment models, each incorporating push or pull at the core:

1. **Direct Selling** is a push function and is not for the timid or faint of heart. Generally one must make an outbound effort to sell. This is a hunter's job rather than a farmer's job. This is the method most frequently used by chambers of commerce and associations with commissioned sales staff. Direct selling can be fast, targeted, and effective.

2. **Marketing** is a pull function, hopefully attracting prospects like insects to a light. If marketing is an organization's primary member recruitment strategy, the marketing material, electronic or print, must be so compelling that it causes a person to, on their own, mail in their membership application, apply on your website, or call the headquarter office to give their credit/debit card number. Marketing is popular among large organizations with substantial budgets.

3. **Member-Get-a-Member** approach is both push and pull as both sales and marketing aspects are included. Members doing the recruiting need the marketing materials for guidance and they also need the association's brand to have a positive meaning within the industry. They can then persuade, in fact sell, their friends, colleagues, suppliers, and competitors to become members. The member-get-a-member approach is often championed by mid-sized and smaller organizations.

Each of the above recruitment methods can be reasonably effective individually, based on resource investment, yet each is not appropriate for every membership organization. Many organizations will select a combination of the above or create hybrid models.

Which Model is Right for You?

If your organization has lots of dollars to spend for member recruitment via sales or marketing, and can afford a very high cost per acquired member, an organic grassroots member recruitment effort just might be too much work. If you have done the cost-benefit analysis of marketing for members or paying commissions, and you are pleased with the results, I'd suggest you continue on that selected course. There are plenty of great sales organizations and marketing companies which specialize in membership organizations that will gladly help you to spend your money.

Interestingly enough, some recent surveys reveal that direct marketing is not as effective as it once was, especially using the conduit of printed materials mailed to prospective members as opposed to more grassroots type efforts. While all association executives have a fiduciary responsibility to spend their members' money wisely, sometimes complacency causes waste. If your organization does not have the marketing dollars or has been disappointed with past results from direct selling or fancy and expensive marketing for member campaigns, perhaps an organic grassroots member recruitment campaign is worth another look.

Method Challenges

While direct selling is the most expedient method for member recruitment, with it comes a price—time and money. In direct selling which includes in-person, door-to-door, telemarketing or even telethons, an organization generally needs commissioned sales persons—hunters. The up side is immediate results but the down side generally is low member retention. The chance for quality member assimilation, or on-boarding, is not as good as member-get-a-member. The reason is numbers—a few people selling a lot of memberships. Those few people are just that—too few for effective member assimilation.

For successful direct selling, employing professional sales persons is generally the only sustainable method. As such, sales people believe their job is to sell, not hand-hold.

Hand-holding is a necessary part of new member assimilation. Also the number challenge comes into play with telethon events. Recruiting 50 members in a day is very possible, but where are the volunteers to help these 50 new people to effectively become part of your organization?

Direct marketing via print or electronic media can be marginally effective and may not deliver the necessary return on your investment. The idea is to do less arm twisting and more "pulling" of potential members to your organization. The pull of marketing can have the exact same challenge as direct selling: effective member assimilation. Too many organizations are just after the dollars or the numbers and neglect to focus on assimilating new members, the individuals or companies.

Author's Personal Story

I recently joined an organization through their email marketing effort. It took them over a month to get a new member information package to me. About a month after that, I still had not had any interaction with a member. I emailed a person listed in the organization's emails and stated that I'd like to get involved. I got an email back that they were busy and would get with me the following month...they finally contacted me a month after that. Will I maintain my membership after the first year? Who knows? You most likely have your own "similar" story. This is a typical scenario for new members of organizations that occur daily. This does not have to be. We can all do better.

Member-Get-a-Member is not without its challenges. This is the preferred approach because the cost is minimal, but the human power is extensive. The prospect is sold and is assimilated effectively. However, if your organization is lacking in person-power or passion, either can quickly become a road block. For members to be truly engaged in this effort, they must be passionate about their organization and the work it does. They must see, understand, and value the benefits they receive from the features of membership.

These brave souls are the ones referred to as ***Member Recruitment Evangelists***. Not having effective recruitment tools for these members is the quickest way to kill their passion. Nevertheless, Member-Get-a-Member campaigns are effective for more membership organizations than any other method.

How your organization approaches growth will largely determine results. If the instant gratification of an immediate membership spike is important to your organization, you will ultimately develop more detractors than evangelists. However, if your organization is willing to adopt an organic grassroots approach to growth, the benefit received by the organization and its members will be transformational. Take this path and your organization will enjoy legions of ***Member Recruitment Evangelists*** in its ranks. Your organization will also enjoy higher than normal member retention—evangelists stay, while detractors leave.

Embarrassingly Enough...

Embarrassingly enough, throughout the early years of conducting member ROI valuation sessions, we thought that was enough to help associations jump-start their member recruitment effort—that was a mistake—it wasn't enough. After watching organizations obtain their real-dollar membership ROI numbers and not use the information well, or even use it at all, frustration kicked in and we realized associations and societies needed much more—they needed a complete plan.

The member recruitment campaign described below is that final puzzle piece—the actionable plan. It's simple to understand and implement, is quite effective, but takes hard work to achieve results. The plan will not administer itself. A strong working partnership among the paid staff and volunteer leaders will serve your organization well. You can do this—you really can. The key here is not to let the process lag due to a bankruptcy of leadership, resources, time, energy and passion.

Your Four-Step Organic Grassroots Member Recruitment Campaign

The idea of a grassroots member recruitment campaign should excite you. It's organic, cost-effective, time-effective, and results-driven. The four basic overview steps listed below will give you a good idea of how you too can develop your own organic grassroots member recruitment campaign:

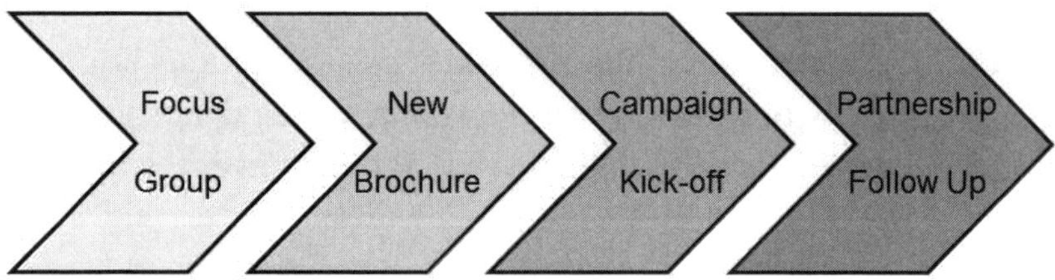

Figure 12

Campaign Step 1:

Do the qualitative research work; conduct the *Rigsbee Member ROI Valuation Process™* for determining the yearly sustainable real-dollar *ROI of Membership* at a meeting, seminar or event with a broad range of members in attendance as discussed in detail in Chapter 4. The results of this work will be the cornerstone upon which you will build your organic campaign. The importance of this first step cannot be stressed enough. But you are already a believer if you have read this far, and must be ready to make this idea work for your association.

Campaign Step 2:

Build the brochure—produce a *dazzle them with brilliance rather than baffle them with bulk* member recruitment brochure; a simple tri-fold that fits in a #10 envelope that has been developed based on the Member ROI Valuation Process™ results. Below is a blueprint for a brochure that works. There are reasons for the placement of information based on how a member might sit with a prospective member and walk them through the information. It is really a step-by-step guide with the most important information offered first. However, you may have very good reasons for creating your brochure with a different layout. If you do change the layout, it is highly suggest you maintain the final (folded) dimensions of 8.5" x 3.7" or something that will fit in a standard #10 envelope. The ease and flexibility of this size will be appreciated by your members.

1. Suggested brochure format:
   a. 11" x 8.5" six-panel tri-fold
   b. Print as four-color double-sided
   c. You will also want to produce an electronic version in PDF format.

2. Brochure covers, figure 13:
   a. Front cover (panel #3) should state something like, "Membership is a Good Business Decision." or "Membership is a Smart Financial Decision" or "Membership is a Smart Career Decision"
   b. Back cover (panel #2) should offer factual and/or historical information about your organization and complete contact information.

3. Upon opening the brochure, as shown in figure 13, the right side (panel #1), should be the results from your *Member ROI Valuation Process™.* This will prove

that through the features of membership your organization offers—joining is a good business decision.

4. The left side (panel #4) should include, the "What's in it for the member," the various industry stakeholder segments or organization's membership categories, figure 15.

5. Last open (inside), figure 15:
    a. Far left (panel #4): What's in it for the individual
    b. Center page (panel #5): What's in it for your business
    c. Right section (panel #6): What's in it for your industry? This is the place for your organization to toot its legislative and advocacy prowess horn. This is because, from a non-member perspective, they are already getting this value even though they do not hold membership in your organization.

The forthcoming examples, figures 14 and 16, are typical of an inexpensively produced brochure that is possible. National Tile Contractors Association produced their first brochure after a Rigsbee Member Valuation Process™ session. Use this as a guide for producing something similar to help your members cause explosive growth.

Panel #1: outside left	**Panel #2: outside center**	**Panel #3: outside right**
Results from your *Member ROI Valuation Process*[TM] including all member-only features that were valued and totals.	A bit of history on your organization and all contact information on the bottom.	This is your brochure cover. In addition to your organizations logo on the top, title the brochure: "Membership is a Good Business Decision!"

Figure 13

Figure 14

Panel #4: inside left	**Panel #5: inside center**	**Panel #6: inside right**
What's in it for the prospect personally? Include a paragraph for all member categories—member, allied, supplier, etc.	What's in it for the prospect's business? Skip the features and list benefits (how your organization will make the member's company better.)	What's in it for the prospect's industry? This is the place to tout the organization's legislative and advocacy work. Remember, industry stakeholder benefit from this even if they are not a member.

Figure 15

What's in it for you personally?

Transcend all your industry business relationships from adversary to collaborative through breaking bread at NTCA events and activities.

TILE CONTRACTORS: Build meaningful relationships with industry peers and other related professionals within the tile industry. Learn leadership techniques to improve on the job effectiveness. Get an edge over your competition and distinguish yourself as an industry leader and trend setter.

DISTRIBUTORS: Benefit from an enhanced collaborative effort on successful residential and commercial projects that become possible through your membership and participation. You'll better understand the people and their business philosophies that are your partners in serving home owners, general contractors, and architects and designers. Through superior relationships with tile contractors and industry manufacturers, your industry partners will have a greater propensity to watch out for your best interest in challenging situations where you are absent.

MANUFACTURERS: Benefit from relaxed interaction with your customers and their colleagues. Better understand the needs and thought processes of tile contractors, and distributors. Through participation become a true industry partner.

NTCA is working with all industry stakeholders to continually improve the competitive landscape across the country with informed and timely information on standards and methods. By doing so all involved save time and money.

What's in it for your business?

NTCA's programs and member benefits are designed to help its members and their businesses, to enjoy growth and profitability. This is achieved effectively through association with peers, colleagues and competitors. To its members, NTCA is a good business decision.

NTCA Reference Manual is a highly effective tool designed to help you trouble shoot problems as they arise in the field. Updated throughout the year to keep you informed of the latest standards and methods. It is now available on CD-ROM!

NTCA *TileLetter* and *TileLetter* online. The premier publication and resource guide for tile and stone contractors worldwide. 13 issues of hot technical and business topics. www.tileletter.com

NTCA Free Technical Advice: As a member you are first in line to get the technical advice you need when you call the association staff.

NTCA Technical Education: Over 40 workshops held across the country designed to keep you updated on the latest standards and methods of tile installation.

NTCA Safety Program: NTCA has taken the best of safety programs from across the country and offers it to the membership. Keep safety a top priority.

NTCA Five Star Contractor Program: For members who have achieved a level of excellence your company can become a five star member. A marketing tool designed for tile contractors ready to take their business to the next level.

NTCA Member discounts on products and services. Enjoy the benefits of freight discounts, coupons and vouchers, and other services as a member of NTCA.

NTCA Web-Site Referral: As a member you will be entered into the NTCA database and website. Let this marketing tool work for you. Homeowners, general contractors, architects and designers can contact you for business. Become linked to NTCA.

What's in it for your industry?

NTCA works hard with industry partners to assure there will be future skilled craftsman for the tile industry.

NTCA has partnered with the Ceramic Tile Education Foundation to support training and education within the tile industry. By recognizing this as an industry function, NTCA, CTEF, Tile Council of North America and other related industry professionals have joined together to address the need for training and education.

The NTCA workshop continues to evolve. Over 40 workshops are held around the country each year to educate the tile contractors and installers as well as their employees. These workshops offer the latest in tile installation methods and standards.

Individuals are recognized each year at the annual meeting called Total Solutions. NTCA recognizes the Tile Person of the Year as well as the Ring of Honor recipients. These awards recognize industry professionals for their commitment to the tile industry.

Industry Relationships

NTCA has established relationships with other industry associations and trade groups. Working together on seminars, conferences and conventions helps keep the tile industry strong.

NTCA is dedicated to Education for Professional Installation. Whether your a tile contractor, distributor, manufacturer, architect, or designer NTCA members receive the very latest information regarding tile installation.

Figure 16

Campaign Step 3:

For a dramatic grassroots launch, build passion for the campaign kick-off at your convention, annual meeting, or other industry wide event with an emotionally charged keynote (meeting opener) revolving around the topic of explosive growth through strategic alliances. Alliance development is the all-important seventh measure in ASAE's seminal book, *7 Measures of Success*. The book focuses on association growth and your members are focused on their growth—both are in concert with one another.

Contact your favorite speaker's bureau or visit the "speaker search page" at the National Speakers Association website at http://www.nsaspeaker.org for a speaker that specializes in strategic alliance development. It might also be helpful to secure a keynote speaker that is both expert in alliance development and member recruitment.

During this alliance keynote presentation, the speaker should close the presentation with a discussion about how your association as actually an industry-wide alliance that delivers high-level value to members. Particularly important in this ending segment is for the speaker to explain how a stronger association can better help members to grow their business or careers. The speaker should get members and other attendees excited about what is possible for themselves and their businesses resulting from a stronger association or society.

After your members understand the benefits they will receive from belonging to a larger organization, it is also the speaker's job to encourage your members to become ***Member Recruitment Evangelists***. During this campaign kick-off keynote the speaker announces the new membership recruitment campaign and asks for a commitment from each member to personally give out ten brochures to colleagues and industry participants. The speaker conducts a reverse "member recruitment altar call" and the board members and staff comes from the back of the room, handing out “batches of ten” member recruitment brochures to each attendee. The majority of your members in attendance will commit to do this and you should expect about 20% to follow through on their own—even more with a small follow up effort from board members.

Another small touch, keeping the pride/prestige buying motive at top of mind—if a member gets another member to join, they are then truly a ***Member Recruitment Evangelist*** and your organization could possibly produce a business size or just a bit larger, card with the members-only features information suggested in a previous chapter. You would also include the evangelist's name on the card and give him/her a prestigious title. Perhaps create a title like, Evangelist Ambassador or something that honors their value to the organization? The staff could send a few cards to the member and suggest they keep the cards readily available, as they are now a proven “Evangelist Ambassador.” Let’s talk emotional ownership—this person is sure to have it now.

Campaign Step 4:

Keep fueling the fire. To do this there are three basic activities that will need constant attention from your organization’s professional staff and your volunteer leaders.

- Work to increase *The ROI of Membership.*
- Support current ***Member Recruitment Evangelists***.
- Work diligently to create new ***Member Recruitment Evangelists***.

An additional value to your organization of the above four-step grassroots recruitment campaign is that it also works in parallel as a member retention campaign with very little additional effort. By raising the question of value, current members are reminded why they have decided to make their positive membership buying decision each year.

Board-Driven Acceleration

Your organization's board of directors and paid staff must review each of the specific features of membership value resulting from your qualitative research valuation process. Next, they must also determine if more low-cost, high-value services and products can be offered to members under the most valued categories. Your board then approves the changes and allows paid staff to implement. Paid staff and the board of directors also start to work on improving member retention through better member engagement using technology to increase capabilities and by developing new areas of member-only value. Start building alliances and affinity programs that will deliver an accelerated *ROI of Membership*. Be careful not to be lulled into the mistake of thinking non-revenues generation and high member value through affinity programs will easily work hand-in-hand. You can enjoy one but rarely both.

> ***Special Note:*** *It is okay to add valuable features of membership after the member recruitment brochure is printed. Don't wait to print the brochure for impending or potential member ROI increases. Get it done now. You know how long it can take for some boards to move forward. These brochures are very inexpensive to print. Keep adding ROI to membership and in a couple years do the qualitative research focus group again. You can then print more brochures with the new and improved numbers. Even if you have several hundred of the old brochures left. Print the new ones and toss the old ones. We are not talking about that*

> *much money—your organization can afford it—do not be caught asleep at the wheel.*

Your board of directors, in collaboration with the paid staff, must drive the campaign. To keep the momentum going, a communication tree needs to be developed where the directors and possibly the membership committee divide the membership for follow-up calls. Calls to members that were in attendance at the strategic alliance presentation should be made approximately 30 days after the meeting. The purpose is to inquire about the members' recruitment results, offer additional member recruitment brochures, and/or to follow up with very interested prospects. No pressure, just a friendly follow-up and an offer of assistance from the chief elected officer and chief staff executive, if necessary. Additionally, the organization's chief elected executive could be asked to send some hand-written notes to some of the members who were making a difference. Getting any of the officers involved in sending hand-written notes thanking evangelists who produce is huge!

It is also important for the board to have a clear understanding of the membership lifecycle model so they can intercede when necessary in areas of the association governance that might be inhibiting the membership experience, and diminishing the ***Member Recruitment Evangelist*** mindset.

The Art and Science of Member Evangelism

The Evangelistic Member Lifecycle Model

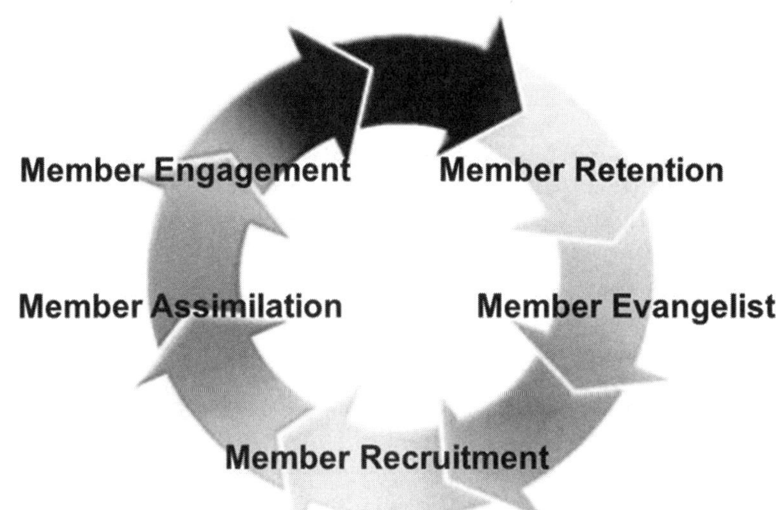

Figure 17

Ultimately you would like each and every member to graduate through this cycle (figure 17) from newly recruited member to ***Member Recruitment Evangelist***. This would surely be the ideal scenario that every membership organization leader, paid or volunteer, would prefer.

1. Starting at the bottom—**Member Recruitment:** the member joins the organization because of their own effort or that of a current member or staff person. They joined to be part of something bigger than themselves, to network, and/or to gain industry specific knowledge and skills. This first stage is a very delicate one. This is where *Relationship Gaps* form without intent. If they cannot easily find the value that caused them to join, they may never assimilate.

In order to move into the next phase, your new member information package must arrive in a timely fashion and must be complete with easy to follow directions for getting involved with the organization.

2. **Member Assimilation:** the member starts to participate; feels welcome, and encouraged to enjoy more of the features of membership that are available to them.

3. **Member Engagement:** the member starts to actively participate on their own accord without the prodding of their mentor, recruiter, or staff person. They are now enjoying many of the benefits that the features of membership offer.

4. **Member Retention:** the member is fully engaged in the organization and has been for several years. They continually see the value that their membership brings both to them and their company. They understand that they get a great return on their investment. They are honored and thanked for their key role in recruitment.

5. **Member as Evangelist:** the member is so thrilled with his or her long-term experience that they want to spread the good news about the benefits of participation. They understand that much of the value they receive is delivered through member-only features offered by their organization and urge others to receive similar value through membership.

6. Coming full-circle—**Member Recruitment:** it all starts again, see step number one.

At the core of your organization's culture, there needs to be a shift in understanding the real-dollar *ROI of Membership*. Everyone needs to understand that your organization delivers true value. This is the basis for recruiting the younger generations that are dealing with working spouses, high-level involvement with their children, and the knowledge that they can seek industry information quite effectively through the Internet. Your organization competes with Google and other search engines every day.

Your organization might consider abandoning its costly "sacred cow" activities in favor of developing high-value communities of reciprocity and other desirable activities for members of all ages...and engaging contrarian members too. Prove to current and new members alike that holding membership in your organization is a good business decision.

At the core of your organization's culture, there needs to be a shift in understanding the real-dollar ROI of Membership

Shift Your Culture to Member Recruitment Evangelism

Arguably, culture trumps strategy, data, experience and knowledge. If this is so, then culture should be very high on your punch-list. To change your organization's culture to one of collaboration—both staff and member stakeholders must be willing to see and accept a new path and partner with one another for the betterment of the organization.

Through extensive research for *The Art of Partnering* the idea of internal collaboration in alliance development and implementation is crucial. Partnering starts in the executive suite and emanates from that point concentrically. The chief staff executive must be completely on-board with the idea of interdepartmental partnering for member recruitment and supporting the efforts of the ***Member Recruitment Evangelists***. This culture shift drive must be done daily.

Staff Culture

Interdepartmental partnering challenges are very real. You've seen it—one department is leading the recruitment and retention charge and another is building the barriers to keep people out—both are working at cross-purposes and wasting their time and resources.

If you are going to create a culture of collaboration, consider:

1. **Dissent**, which is the sentiment or philosophy of non-agreement or opposition to a prevailing idea. This is common in organizations with silo mentality and fiefdoms. In these circumstances, effective member recruitment is at threat.

2. **Cooperation**, which is the process of getting along through compromise or abdication. In this situation, the dictate has been sent down from Mount High, or the CSE, that everyone must get along. This is where toleration is the accepted strategy.

3. **Collaboration**, which is the process of creating higher productivity or innovation through synergistic efforts. In this environment, everyone wants to work with one another for a common result.

The staff members' job isn't to do all the member recruitment themselves but to celebrate members who are passionate about their membership. Collaborative staff can be recruitment-infectious when sharing tools and support with members. Collaborative staff members realize that members getting things done, recruiting new members, a different way can be just fine. When you build a culture of collaboration you will foster your culture of ***Member Recruitment Evangelism***.

Author's Personal Story

While I was working on the second draft of this book, I was engaged to present a keynote to a CEO group at a medical industry convention. Having an extra couple hours before I had to leave, I did my usual walk of the exposition floor. I noticed a professional society that had a booth intended to promote membership in their organization.

Since I had done a fair amount of qualitative research work with this very large society, I clearly knew their real-dollar member ROI number. I couldn't resist—I asked the two staffers working the booth, "If I joined your society, how many dollars back in value would I receive for each dollar invested in membership?" They both were dumbfounded and stated that they couldn't answer my question. I rebutted, "That's interesting. I can tell you how much. I did the research and wrote the article answering this question for your organization."

Here is my point; get your staff on board and up to speed on membership ROI and its value in recruitment. In that very large society, the various departments truly have the silo mentality. I was hired by the marketing department to conduct the research. When the marketing department asked the publishing department to run the article that I wrote, detailing the real-dollar ROI numbers of membership in their magazine—the publishing department refused. The marketing department had to pay to have the article run as an advertisement. And worse, the real-dollar ROI of membership numbers got lost in this behemoth organization. The departments worked at cross-purposes. You surely can do better.

Member Culture

Depending on the industry or profession, it is not uncommon for members to desire to keep competitors from joining and receiving the benefits available through membership. Help your long-term members to see the wisdom behind diversity and inclusion, especially in the generational area. Help prevent the fear of young upstarts or competitors. Help your current members see the value to them personally in your organization's effort to reach membership critical mass. While you are at it, encourage your younger, committed leaders to reach out to long-term members to tap their wisdom and experience. Once your organization speaks for the industry majority, and values young and old alike, everyone listens. That alone is an excellent reason for a culture of ***Member Recruitment Evangelism***.

Evangelism—What's In It for the Baby Boomers?

- **Legacy:** the senior members of your organization see retirement closer than before, and their thoughts emerge about leaving footprints. Help them to see and satisfy the need for their life's work to matter and to continue.

- **Making a difference:** when senior members mentor younger members, both win. The senior member gets the satisfaction of moving from simply being successful to living significantly, while the junior member accelerates their industry learning curve through accessing the senior member's lifetime knowledge bank.

- **Legislative power:** your senior members have strong opinions on their industry and the role government plays in enabling or inhibiting commerce. Greater representation matters. The more market share your organization represents within your industry, the greater the voice your organization will have locally, regionally, and nationally. This will be more of a motivator for the evangelist than the new member. Be certain to keep your evangelists focused on *The ROI of Membership.*

- **More programs:** with more members comes more money to focus on the specific and special interest needs of various contingency groups represented by your organization—and hopefully some of the new programs developed will be focused on the needs of senior members.

- **Successful succession planning:** senior members, in many cases, plan to turn their business over to the next generation. Leaving behind, a strong and thriving association bolsters their confidence that the next generation will have the knowledge, tools, and skills necessary for effective company leadership and governance.

Evangelism—What's In It for the Other Generations?

- While some of the benefits of association growth will be similar for all the generations, the most convincing argument for the younger generations will be economies of scale—meaning, more members equals more dollars and more dollars should mean more and higher quality features of membership. With increased membership dollars and numbers, simply more of everything, hopefully good, is possible.

All Association Members Must Become Evangelists

Perhaps it's a fool's errand to attempt to get all members to become evangelists, nevertheless help your members to understand that if they expect the organization to serve them well; they too must become actively engaged in member recruitment evangelism. They must be willing to sing from the rooftops *The ROI of Membership*. Teach your members to tell all their colleagues, competitors, and suppliers why they too should become members.

While this is not a widely embraced perspective, it is the chief staff executive's job to drive the vision and a continual membership recruitment campaign. What's important to the CSE is important to the organization. Staff and volunteer leaders are "watching" what the CSE does far more than they are "listening" to what he/she says. Realize that the more everyone understands and appreciates the true ROI of membership, the easier it will be for them to share that appreciation with those that they are trying to recruit into the organization.

Teach your members to tell all their colleagues, competitors, and suppliers why they too should become members

Messaging topics for ***Member Recruitment Evangelists*** might include:

- Join our association and let us help you to be more profitable through our member-only benchmark cost saving studies, leading-edge business development education and peer-to-peer mentoring programs. Our members have told us that mentoring program alone is worth $2,000 a year.

- Join our society and enjoy the comfort and peace of mind of knowing that you will receive up to the minute member-only legislative and regulatory updates which will assuredly keep you from running afoul with industry regulators and watchdog organizations. If they were to pay a staffer to find this information in a timely manner, members have told us it would take a minimum of 60 hours a year. Multiply that times the gross cost of a staffer at your practice and you will have a real-dollar savings number.

- Join our association and increase your market share through the Internet business leads that are a feature of membership. Our newer members have told us that they have increased revenues by 20% in the first year.

Your organization should be a wonderful, industry-wide strategic alliance enabling all stakeholders to harness the collective strength of an industry and thereby receiving the value proposition they need. The members, who are actively involved as functionaries in their industry, rather than the suppliers, should be the ones driving an association's member recruitment.

Your paid staff members already get their benefit—a paycheck. This statement is not meant to diminish the role of paid staff. However, there is a different dynamic between the persons who are *pay-to-play* members and associate members, versus the ones who are *paid-to-work*—the staff. The times when the paid staff working at your organization experience this *pay-to-play* dynamic is mostly if they participate in organizations like ASAE, State SAEs, MPI, and PCMA where they, too, are paying members.

The suppliers always get a huge amount of value from participation—networking with their customers. However, it is the functionary (regular) member that stands to gain the most through participation so it behooves them to lead the member recruitment charge.

Suppliers are Members Too

At this point it needs to be stated that suppliers or affiliate members should be able to participate in the association and should be permitted to hold board positions. However, there are too many associations addicted to the opiate of having their suppliers do all the work in driving their industry's association. It is not their job—it's the job of the regular members! Suppliers will happily do all the work, but by relinquishing regular member responsibility this abdication will only weaken the organization and its member recruitment efforts.

What about Staff?

Train all staff to become recruiters. Train them with similar messaging topics like previously mentioned. Sure, their job is to enable, support, and encourage the membership—and yet, they can do more. If a prospective member calls or emails an inquiry, teach them to instantly jump on it and get out the member recruitment brochure. Hopefully similar to what was outlined earlier. Teach them to forward critical inquiries to the volunteer membership committee to close the deal—or it could be vice versa—that's okay too. If staff does their job and does not function as a stumbling block and sheds the silo mentality, then there is no excuse—every serious inquiry should be converted to membership. If your staff knows your members well, encourage them to offer to introduce potential new members to others who have a similar background or profile. That connection can serve to close the loop and help connect them to a member who can help bring them into the community and keep them involved. However, if the paid staff is too busy doing the work that the volunteer leaders and their committees should be doing, they will not instantly jump on membership inquiries, and potential members will be lost.

Staff Enablers

Association staff members are in a unique position to be either a ***Member Recruitment Evangelist*** enabler or encumbrance. The issue at stake might be one of control—whose association is it? Another issue might be concerns about sharing the workload or areas of accountability. When your staff says the members are not doing their job, you need to explore the accusation. If correct, ask why and repair the situation using the chief staff executive as your point person. If the indictment is baseless, you have to straighten out your house (headquarters) immediately.

When a potential member contacts the association office, this is gold. Does your organization have a sense of urgency among the association staff to respond quickly? While the correct method of handling inquiries, staff-driver or volunteer-driven, is up to individual organizations to decide, speed should not be up for debate.

What about recognition? Something as simple as evangelism acknowledgement, perhaps in your newsletter a personalized Evangelist Ambassador business card, or some other communication, can go a long way to encourage your members to become ***Member Recruitment Evangelist***. Let's be clear on the idea; the suggestion is **recognition, not incentive!**

Volunteer versus Staff-Driven Evangelism

This is a frequent question: "Who leads the charge?" Is it the professional staff, the volunteers or both? Today this question may be more crucial than ever before. Let's explore what each side brings to the member recruitment, assimilation and retention evangelistic table.

Staff-Driven Recruitment Effort:

- **Reliability:** long-term performance will generally have a stronger chance with staff. They tend to get things done especially when it is their primary job. When member recruitment is part of an employee's job description, there is a strong survival motivation to do the work of recruitment. Contrast this with a busy member stating that they have been busy running their own business. If it is a staff person's job, they'll usually get it done.

- **Consistency:** when member recruitment is one's job, or part of it, there will generally be a more methodical and consistent outreach effort and better organizational knowledge to aid in the effort. With staff, one might consider there will be less likelihood that things will fall through the cracks.

- **Clear message:** communicating a clear message is expected from the professional staff. Their recruitment message will be scripted and benefit-driven. Making multiple calls daily will allow professionals to hone their sales message, making their communication more easily understood.

- **Dedicated resources:** generally headquarters staff will have more member recruitment marketing materials available on a daily basis than would members. Having regular access to all the latest and greatest brochures and other member recruitment tools that your organization produces improves success rates. With great management, staff will also have a scheduled amount of time daily that they will dedicate to making recruitment outreach and sales calls.

- **Knowledge:** generally a staff person, working the member recruitment effort daily, will have a greater understanding of the organization's features of membership and how the prospective member can utilize those features to make them valuable benefits for their business or career.

- **Outsider perspective:** looking at the organization from the staff perspective is much different than from that of the members. This different perspective is usually clear of industry jading and erroneous perceptions. Having the larger overview perspective can be of substantial benefit in member recruitment success.

Communicating a clear message is expected from the professional staff

Volunteer-Driven Recruitment Effort

- **Authenticity:** members are perceived as more authentic in their evangelism because their recruitment efforts will come primarily from the heart rather than the brain. Further, the emotional connection to an industry colleague will be dramatically more powerful than that of an office staff person with a highly scripted message—that might come off too slick.

- **Peer-to-peer:** members will have easier access to colleagues within the industry and also command a high-level of credibility.

- **Word-of-mouth:** members can create an industry buzz through their suppliers and customers about the great value membership offers. Because members are generally geographically dispersed, the potential for a *blanket of industry* interaction is far greater than would be possible for the headquarter staff to achieve.

- **Greater numbers:** there are far more people available on the member side. Consider the member recruitment effectiveness from hundreds of volunteers geographically dispersed and talking to colleagues. This will deliver more industry in-person touches than would be possible for staff.

- **Personalized examples:** storytelling is gold in selling. Member examples deliver unequaled persuasive power when using the association enabled, personal success stories. Members can explain from doing, rather than observing, how their trade association or professional society helps them to solve problems, access business opportunities, or other delivered membership features that create a high level *ROI of Membership* to them personally or to their business. They have stories that sell and inform.

- **Industry jargon:** naturally someone that is actively participating in his or her industry will have a deeper understanding of insider industry speak. This makes the job of the **Member Recruitment Evangelist** quite a bit easier. The exception may be a long-term association employee. However, by the time an employee is high-level knowledgeable, he or she will most likely be in a top executive position. Unfortunately, executive staff is rarely involved in daily member recruitment efforts.

- **Passion:** the member who truly understands and appreciates the benefit value that his or her association delivers through the features of membership will have the propensity to become a true ***Member Recruitment Evangelist***.

Members can create an industry buzz through their suppliers and customers about the great value membership offers

The Partnership Model

The answer to staff or member-driven recruitment is a hybrid model based on both staff and volunteer resources of the organization. Every organization is different, although every organization should want to take advantage of staff and members working in partnership. Both bring strengths to the table. The challenge for many organizations is this; very few paid staffers will ever become true ***Member Recruitment Evangelists***. Let's be real. For staff, no matter how dedicated—it's a job. For a member—it could be their livelihood, career or legacy.

However, it is also true that not every officer or board will be equally committed to member recruitment. In that case, the association staff members are the long-term glue that keeps the process going through the good and bad times. In the good times, they are ready to hand it off and applaud the members making a difference. In the lean years, they are there to pick up the ball and run with it.

Collaboration is still possible. Both staff and members each have their own motivation for member recruitment. The savvy CSE can help activate all the reasons and motivation for performance, thereby getting staff and members to work hand-in-hand to achieve the organizational member recruitment goals.

Which side should take the lead? It does not matter as long as staff and members are working in harmony. The size or your organization's membership and staff might dictate which side takes the lead. The key is an organized and detailed plan listing responsibilities. Have a contingency plan for staff or board vacancies. Do not let the momentum die because of some foreseeable challenge. There needs to be a custodian, the keeper of the idea, a person that will lead the charge and motivate everyone involved. The CSE could very well be that person.

There is one warning; when staff takes the lead, and is primarily focused on numbers, be wary. The scenario that frequently follows is that staff drives quantity before quality and is bankrupt of effective member assimilation tactics. If this happens, the current and generally long-time members will perceive that their organization is going south very quickly—and many of these valuable people might jump ship. When staff takes the lead, there should be incentives in place for staff to help retain each member for no less than five years. An assimilation strategy must be in place.

Build Your Brand

For your members to be effective ***Member Recruitment Evangelists***, they must have a crystal clear understanding of the organizational brand in their own minds. This is crucial before they can eloquently articulate the virtues of membership to the non-believers. Your association is a brand, both in the minds of members and that of non-members. To members the brand has a particular meaning—most likely very positive and comforting.

To the non-member though, what meaning does the brand hold? How would you even know? The brand must not have much of a meaning at all in the mind of the non-member. If it did, and was positive, they would have already joined and become a member. When a non-member states that membership is too expensive, what they are really saying is, "I do not see the value." If they do not see the value, whose fault is it—theirs? Not by a long-shot. It is the responsibility of your organization to clearly and succinctly define the brand and the member value proposition. If the brand has a negative connotation in the minds and hearts of non-members, effective member recruitment is very difficult—at best.

Brand means so much more than just a logo. Everything matters from the look of your website and your social media online presence to the beauty, feel and energy of your headquarters office to the kind of people and organizations that hold membership. Your association brand, perceived by members and non-members alike, is the total of all that you are, do, and represent. Who in your industry that chooses to participate, and does not, is an important indicator to many about the organization's strength and vitality—or the lack of. When industry high-level and influential people participate in your organization, it sends a clear message of value to the industry at large.

What can you do to make your brand more powerful in the minds of your industry? Start by deciding who and what you are. Then drive the vision by both word and deed. Last, let it be clear to one and all in the industry just how your organization will make their life better through its features of membership. Nothing adds more meat to the bones of your brand than a powerful membership ROI process and ongoing-campaign.

Your association is a brand, both in the minds of members and that of non-members

Show Evangelists the Money

If you don't tell them, they cannot know you did it. This is called Documented Value Added. Simply put, when you do something for another— something that they consider as being valuable to them—you had better tell them that you did it or in their mind, you never did. Every time you or one of your staff members helps an association member, take a moment to write and mail that member a note thanking them for the opportunity to serve. Mention specifically what you did for them, the service provided. Effectively you are documenting the Value Added your members receive.

Here is an example, *"Dear Member, thank you for the opportunity to help you overcome your code challenge (or anything you did for them). It was heart-warming to know that we at the National XYZ Association were able to overcome the $5,000 fine that the local municipality wanted to impose."*

Some organizations send out an invoice for the service—as can yours. They list a "member discount" equaling the dollar value of the service/help rendered to a zero balance. Show them the money and lock in their desire to remain a member. There is also a strong likelihood that they will share their "How I saved money" story with someone in the industry that is not yet a member of your association—that's a good thing. ***Member Recruitment Evangelists*** can be developed easier than you might think.

Evangelists & Incentives

Do you really need to give your members a $25 Starbucks card to motivate them to tell a colleague or competitor why *it is a good business decision* to hold membership in your organization? Giving current members an incentive for recruiting new members can be a great way to temporarily boost membership numbers but is a poor method for true organizational organic growth. This is similar to a sales person that is only interested in making the sale and not interested in developing long-term customers. Instant gratification is rarely the best course of action for sustainable organizational growth.

The true long-term organizational value derived from an aggressively competitive recruiting member is generally minimal. This is because the effort is solely for his or her ego and need for the instant gratification of winning a contest. Can, or will, this aggressively competitive recruiter also aggressively help to assimilate the new recruits—probably not. Without successful assimilation, there will be very little retention.

Just to name a few—monetary, gift, or travel incentives—are not ideal for member recruitment in the long-term. Give your ***Member Recruitment Evangelists*** plenty of recognition, publicly and privately. The monetary cost to the organization will be negligible. That, and other benefits mentioned earlier, will generally be all that the true evangelist needs.

Conversely, the incentive-driven recruitment delivers a turnstile of members, wastes valuable resources and ultimately damages an organization's reputation. Rather than having advocates and ***Member Recruitment Evangelists*** in the marketplace praising the benefits of membership, turnstile member recruitment fosters disgruntled ex-members that extol the perceived indifference that they experienced while holding membership. They talk about the lack of ROI and the benefits they didn't receive. In this situation, your organization would have been better off not having had them as members in the first place.

Instant gratification is rarely the best course of action for sustainable organizational growth

Evangelists' Role in New Member Assimilation

Your new members receive huge value from attending your conventions and conferences, even more so when they have a guide and mentor serving as their pathfinder. This is an activity which evangelists embrace. The challenge with the above-mentioned incentive-driven membership recruiter is that said recruiter has no time to be a pathfinder for several freshman members. Sometimes organizations are sophisticated enough to assign first-time conference attendees a mentor, but this is only minimally effective without a prior relationship.

The absolute best member recruitment strategy for effective new member assimilation is one member gets one new member each year. The member can more successfully urge the new member to attend the organization's upcoming conference and serve as their pathfinder and assimilator throughout the meeting. The new member feels included, receives benefit from educational and networking opportunities, and develops an emotional ownership in their membership. This is the crucial foundation for any long-term member.

The absolute best member recruitment strategy for effective new member assimilation is one member gets one new member each year

Changing Member Recruiters' Motivation

To transform your members from aggressive recruiters solely motivated on the instant gratification of winning a contest or filling their pockets with incentives into strong advocates and hopefully, evangelists, takes smart planning and implementation strategies. Your current members must truly understand and believe, to their core, that their association or society delivers an excellent return on their investment of both money and time.

They must have a strong emotional ownership in the idea that *membership is a good business decision.* They must also understand how a larger and stronger organization will have the capability to deliver even more measurable value to every stakeholder. There is always the fear that if the organization grows too much the intimacy will disappear. The organization must also demonstrate through its long-term planning strategy that there are future programs being developed to sustain the valued intimacy.

Converting the Contrarian Member to Evangelism

Your contrarian members, the ones you currently consider to be a pain in the neck or a thorn in your side and really wish would leave—are almost always passionate persons who see the world, its patterns and trends, differently from most. They are simply waiting to be acknowledged and invited to participate. They will want to participate in a way that works for them—nevertheless, they want to participate. Contrarians are energetic and vigorous. If they are passionate about something they will devote their entire being toward that resolve. If you want your contrarians to have an emotional ownership in your member recruitment campaign or any other activity, the solution is simple. Don't fear them. Include them and collaborate with them—why not harness this passionate energy and their legitimate strengths for the good of the association?

It is your job as the association executive to harness their passion and to figure out how to *herd these cats* in ways that serve both the organization in general and the contrarian in specific. There is room for some sort of middle ground, for some kind of balance between loving and hating contrarian members. It's all about perception—the perception of the disengaged contrarian as to how they are *feeling* or *believing.* With a modicum of effort, association leaders like you can quite easily engage your contrarians through inclusiveness. If you have the ability to be a forward thinker, to explore how something might be achieved, rather than holding tight to beliefs as to why something cannot be done, you can engage these individuals. Contrarians could prove to be your greatest allies and provide valuable input.

It's unfortunate that contrarians are generally thrown into a single category of malcontents. This is far from being accurate. It takes some detective work on your part to dissect the contrarian membership into various stakeholder categories. This can only be done when you attempt to understand the primary issues various contrarians have with exclusion, perceived or real, by their association. Honest discourse is the answer to discovering the true issues that cause contrarian disengagement. Next, and this is an absolute, an honest effort **must** be made by the association to shore up the association's deficiencies in serving its various stakeholder groups. If, through conversations with contrarians or contrarian member groups, deficiencies are uncovered and not addressed, you will most likely lose those contrarian members and they will become vocal, disgruntled non-members—at best. At worst—they might start a competing association or society. The American Medical Association, as mentioned in Chapter 5, has surely experienced this truth. It is always better to have a diverse palette of members fully engaging in receiving and giving value to the association and industry than to have a number of stakeholders leaving or believing they have been left behind.

Similar to the earlier discussion on collaborative staff, transitioning from a silo driven organization to one that values high-level collaboration is not always easy but is always rewarding and usually successful in the long-term. Give up on the idea of ruling the organization with an iron fist. It's not uncommon for outliers or contrarians operating within your organization to create opportunities and activities that might, for many other members, add to the total value of membership. In these kinds of situations, it's frequently far better to collaborate and accept the additional member value than to attempt domination over the membership. If you want your contrarian members to also become ***Member Recruitment Evangelists***, you need to emotionally move past cooperation to collaboration. By collaborating with contrarians, you are offering them a seat at the table. When you truly offer a seat, and don't simply placate, contrarians will become engaged and deliver true member recruitment value to the organization.

This is an absolute, an honest effort must be made by the association to shore up the association's deficiencies in serving its various stakeholder groups

Senior Members & Sacred Cows

Highly engaged long-term members are your first, best hope for explosive growth in member recruitment. Who more than these members, are qualified to sing the praises of *The ROI of Membership* that your organization delivers? These members could and should be easily converted to ***Member Recruitment Evangelists***. Since these members generally can access their non-member colleagues far easier than can the professional headquarters staff, why not make the most of what you've got?

However, these senior members might also be the ones that push and are insistence that the organization maintains certain legacy programs, products and services—commonly known as sacred cows. As mentioned in the Chapter 5 *Member Value/Resource Allocation Framework Process*, these programs can squander your organization's time and treasure resources. The majority of your engaged and retained members are probably Baby Boomers. Their membership paradigm is that of joining their trade association or professional society because they feel the need to support their industry or profession. Yes, those were the good old days for associations—gone perhaps forever. Today, the majority of younger association and society stakeholders, the non-members, are less interested in joining because they should and much more interested in what's in it for them—what's my return on investment? This creates a chasm between the programs, products and services desired by the various generations.

Now is the time to negotiate with your senior members for sunset dates on unnecessary or obsolete programs, services, and products. As younger generations of business leaders and professionals are joining or considering membership, the sacred cow protectors in your organization are experiencing reduced support and thereby are exhibiting lowered resistance to change. They are starting to realize that keeping things as they always were is not a reality—especially when placed under the tight economic microscope. The process itself will help focus their attention on the sacred cows that are now high cost and low value. This process will take them out of opinion and into qualitative data that can often give them the confidence to let go and help invent the future of an association they love and helped create.

If you even have a faint indication that you might be a sacred cow protector, this is the time to let it go. To help you work through the process of either defending or letting go, consider the following:

- Why should this program, product or service continue?
- Who cares most about this program, product or service?
- Why do they protect it?
- Which organizational stakeholder segments does the program, product or service still serve?
- Is this program, product or service still profitable?
- Is this program, product or service worth the organizational resources that are necessary to sustain it?

- Has this program, product or service reached its sunset?

How do you help an ironclad mind to open up? Perhaps oil and leverage will do the trick?

1. The oil relates to the idea of slipperiness versus friction. Their ironclad mind is the friction and you become the oil that helps movement. Your job is to help the protector see that there might be new or better ideas, products and services that might possibly, maybe, perhaps serve the market better than the currently protected sacred cow.

2. Leverage relates to an outside object or force that allows ease of movement for heavy or stuck objects. Needless to say, the stuck or heavy object is the sacred cow protector. The outside force could be higher authority or replacement product/service. Higher authority needs no explanation. Replacement, however, is a formidable subject. Where or what could the cow protector use as an alternate crutch for channeling their passion? Figure that out and you have both oil and leverage available to help you, to help the protector move toward something better.

Senior Concerns & Sacred Cow Killing

The best scenario is to have senior members let go of dead or dying programs and embrace member recruitment in an evangelistic manner. If you can help them, as you did with the contrarians, to focus their energy, passion and desire to leave footprints—you'll have an awesome ***Member Recruitment Evangelist***. Please consider the following:

- Long-term equity is bestowed upon those who have participated through volunteerism for years. These folks also enjoy chronological credibility. However, going up against long-term networks of support is wrought with landmines, especially for younger, innovative, and excited members. The most critical challenge that faces non-profits today is honoring members with this long-term equity while simultaneously defending the emergence of youthful exuberance. Can they both co-exist? Yes, they certainly can.

- Changing member needs and desires compound the above conundrum. This is an area where paid non-profit staff and volunteer leadership must work toward mutually beneficial programs, services and long-term strategic plans to gradually turn the page to a new era. The need for this phenomenon generally occurs every decade or two. As an example, many organizations are now discovering that the sacred cow golf tournament that has always taken place before a convention can no longer sustain itself financially. The old-timers defend it with all the oomph and gusto they can muster but the newer functionaries in the industry do not care. Perhaps the tournament's sunset has arrived?

- Non-profits must be keenly aware of current and emerging competition from non-traditional sectors. There might be products or services your organization has provided to its members since the dawning of time. While there might now be for-profit companies that provide the same, or better, products or services faster, cheaper, and with more choice than your non-profit could ever achieve. Might it be time to slaughter that sacred cow and grind it up into hamburger for all to benefit from and enjoy?

The most critical challenge that faces non-profits today is honoring members with this long-term equity while simultaneously defending the emergence of youthful exuberance

It is important to deliver honest ROI to your members. Equally crucial is to value that which delivers value. Discontinue valueless propositions and needless bottlenecks in your organization will be the life-blood for explosive growth in this new era of member recruitment. You will want to look at what else your organization has of value to offer its members—features of membership that have not been offered in the past. Engage your senior members in this effort.

Take a play from Tim Ellis' playbook—when he was the Chief Marketing Officer for the Los Angeles County Bar Association, he created the "Dinosaur Group" for his senior members. They paid a few extra dollars to belong and received special programing based on their interests and perhaps even more important—they received recognition for their station within the profession. They proudly wore a LACBA membership pin which prominently featured a dinosaur in the center.

Everyone, including the members of your organization, wants to feel like they receive a commensurate value for their time and money investment. Prove to them through qualitative research that they are receiving that value. Then regularly communicate the real-dollar ROI in numbers and useable benefits rather than simply features. Do this and your organization will enjoy explosive growth.

In conclusion, you now have the missing link for explosive growth and agree with, and have an emotional ownership in, the book's opening statement: *Nothing is more effective for influencing the decision to join than proving The ROI of Membership and communicating to non-members, through real-dollar numbers, that membership is a smart career, business, and/or financial decision.* You are now armed with the concepts, tools, and skills to help your organization experience explosive membership growth and effective member retention. There is just one more ingredient necessary and it is totally up to you: **passion**.

Chapter 7 Executive Action Steps:

1. See your organization through the eyes of the non-member. Do not allow yourself to be deceived by the opiate of complacency—believing that all is well and wait for the industry, economy, or whatever to recover. Aggressively dissect your value proposition through the window of non-member perception and continually make the necessary adjustments.

2. Sell the benefits. Benefits are solutions to problems. Everyone wants their problems solved. Very few people buy from a "Features Jockey." Continually focus on the "how this makes the members' life better." Every time you catch yourself saying the "our benefits of membership are..." and then you rattle off the features of membership—**STOP!** Better, is to state the feature of membership and then explain how that feature will make the person's life better.

3. Measure your members' perception of value. Perception is reality. Be concerned with your members' reality, not yours. The more you measure, the easier it is to sell the idea of membership to others. While measuring all-industry benefit activities might be helpful for member retention, it's the member-only features that create the value that non-members will join to receive. The non-member will become a member if they perceive that their return on investment is great enough. Know your real-dollar Membership ROI multiplier and communicate it frequently throughout the industry.

4. Visit www.rigsbee.com/roi7.htm for a video chapter review and additional ideas from the author.

Prologue

From the first draft of this book, the feedback I received from several association executives was, "Give us more." Truth be told, this book was originally positioned more as a book to sell my qualitative research sessions and member recruitment campaigns. However the book morphed into more of a "consultant in a box" kind of book where my attempt in writing was to hold nothing back.

I firmly believe that you have now been armed with the tools and systems, which can easily enable you to prove to your industry or profession that membership in your organization is a smart career, business, and financial decision. You have been given the formula and steps to determine *The ROI of Membership* in your organization based on member-only value determined by your members.

Also, you now have additional membership selling skills and ideas on how to convert your members, all of your members, into ***Member Recruitment Evangelists***. Now it is up to you. What will you do with this newly gained information? Will you place the book on a shelf thinking that you'll get going on the ideas presented here when "things settle down" or will you just make the time to start?

You can decide to be like the unnamed trade association CEO mentioned in Chapter 2, not believing that your organization's member-only programs, products and services are enough to compel membership among the non-believers. I truly hope you decide to be more like Bart Bettiga, Executive Director, at the National Tile Contractors Association who has grown his organization three fold in five years—following our qualitative session and using many of the ideas outlined in this book. For even more help, remember to view the "additional content" videos listed in the *Executive Action Steps* at the end of each chapter.

You may decide to do it all yourself or you may decide to seek professional help in doing the things necessary to grow your organization's membership. Whatever you choose, I believe you can do it now that you have the missing link for explosive growth. Over the past 25 years working with associations, I have met some amazing people that do amazing work. If you believe in yourself, your staff, and volunteers, you will truly be unstoppable.

If you decide to take the route of using professional help, you'll also need to decide on using a local or national consultant and/or facilitator. Throughout this book, there were recommendations on how to seek help. Or, if it makes your life easier, give me a call at 805-498-5720 or send me an email at ed@rigsbee.com and we can talk about your grassroots member recruitment campaign.

One more gift—you may access articles adapted from this book and my other books on alliance development for electronic or print publication at no charge from my article bank at **www.rigsbee.com/morearticles.htm**. Please help yourself. –Ed Rigsbee

Member ROI Summit™

Now that you have read the book, why not treat yourself, your staff, and volunteer leaders to a live event. Jump-start your efforts to increase *The ROI of Membership* and accelerate member recruitment at your organization by attending a Member ROI Summit™. Consider hosting or attending a public event. For a list of upcoming opportunities, visit **www.rigsbee.com/Member_ROI_Summits.htm**.

Rigsbee Research, an approved CAE education provider, conducts Member ROI Summits™ in two formats. The small group format is generally limited to twelve participants. In the small group, attendees benefit from a consultative environment where association and society executives share and learn in a private setting. Here, participants have the opportunity to dive deep into issues that might not be possible in a large group setting.

The other format is a large group which is generally held in partnership with societies of association executives (SAE) or industry specific association executive councils (AEC) without a limit on size. The Member ROI Summit™, in either format, is held as a full-day event providing participants with six CAE approved educational hours.

Glossary of Terms

- **Chief Elected Officer** (CEO) is the top volunteer leader, generally the Chair or President of the board of directors.
- **Chief Staff Executive** (CSE) is the top paid staff person. This person in in charge of all the paid staff and it is their job to liaison with the CEO.
- **Content Marketing** is a twenty-first century term tied close to social media. It is an idea of pulling customers toward an organization by giving away valuable information that might be valuable to the customer.
- **Documented Value Added** is a term used heavily in the distribution industries. It refers to giving a customer more than they anticipated. The value the customer receives is measured and recorded for future negotiations and update sessions with customers.
- **Feature of Membership** is a term used to differentiate in two ways. First, between a product, service or activity that is only available to an individual or company through their membership. Second, it helps to distinguish between a feature which is built into a product or service and the benefit one receives from using or having said product or service.
- **Good of the Order** is where membership organization participants urge others to also participate for the sole reason of benefitting the organization rather than benefiting the member.
- **Group Champion** is an individual that while might not have a title; they are the driving force behind making a group or community successful and valuable to all the participants.

- **Industry Stakeholder Benefit** is what all the members of an industry receive from an organization's (within that industry) good works whether they are a member or not.
- **Knowledge Management** is the process and/or activity of gathering, organizing, and making easily available to members crucial industry codes, regulatory, legislative, best practice, compensation, and other important knowledge.
- **Member-Only Benefit** is the value delivered from various features of membership that are not available to non-members.
- **Passing the Smell Test** is the process of data filtering through the empirical knowledge sensibilities of interested individuals to become accepted knowledge among those same individuals.

About the Author

Ed Rigsbee, CAE, CSP, grew up in Southern California and is no stranger to membership organizations as he started early at 15 years of age by joining a youth fraternity, The Order of DeMolay (Garden Grove, CA), sponsored by the Masonic Lodge. He maintained membership until the age of 21 when he joined the Masonic Lodge (Thousand Oaks, CA) and became an adult advisor for the fraternity. He remained an advisor for about a decade then in the mid-1980s he helped found a Rotary Club (Westlake Village, CA) and served as president 1987-1988.

In 1988 he also joined the National Speakers Association (NSA) as a professional member, receiving the Certified Speaking Professional (CSP) designation in 2000—an accreditation that less than 10% of the Global Speakers Federation membership holds. In the late 1980s he was juggling memberships in Rotary, NSA, and Greater Los Angeles Chapter-NSA (GLAC). In 1991, when his oldest son started youth soccer at age 5, he got involved in the American Youth Soccer Organization (AYSO) Region 9 (Thousand Oaks, CA) as a coach. Later he added refereeing and also served as an executive board member at AYSO Region 9. During that time he also earned a "State" level certification with the United States Soccer Federation. In 2008 he completely retired from soccer.

In 1999, Ed and a friend started a small event at the annual convention of the National Speakers Association that grew to become a 501(c)(3) fundraising powerhouse;

Cigar PEG—Fun through Philanthropy (www.cigarpeg.com) and Ed still serves as CEO and executive director to this day. Along the way, he joined ASAE: the Center for Association leadership and received the Certified Association Executive (CAE) credential in 2012. He is one of a very small number of people internationally that holds both the CAE and CSP.

Today, Ed maintains membership in the Conejo Valley Masonic Lodge (Thousand Oaks), NSA, ASAE, and CalSAE. He is well versed as a volunteer and member in membership organizations both national and local.

On the career side, Ed is one of America's most prolific authors on the subject of Business Growth through Strategic Alliances. He travels internationally as a keynoter, consultant, and/or advisor to world class clients such as DHL, Toyota, 3M, Dun & Bradstreet, Spirit Aerospace, BE Aerospace, George Fischer Signet, Mead, Siemens, Roland, Best Buy, and others in the for-profit area. In the non-profit area, he has worked with numerous professional societies and trade associations (both individual and company membership).

Throughout his career, Ed has gained a wide range of experience that helps him to serve his clients well: retail management positions, outside sales and sales management positions, owned a manufacturer's representative company, and has also served an adjunct professor. Since 1991, he has focused primarily on authoring, professional speaking and consulting activities. This panoramic perspective has propelled him to become a no-nonsense consultant. Ed doesn't tell clients what they want to hear but rather what they need to hear. In 2006 he added professional association management to his professional activities.

His empirical knowledge gained over several decades of professional and volunteer activities has helped Ed to perfect his qualitative research methodology, *The Rigsbee*

Member Valuation Process™, for proving *The ROI of Membership* in real-dollar numbers which he believes is today's missing link for of explosive membership growth.

On a personal note, Ed and his wife, Regina, have resided in Thousand Oaks, California (greater Los Angeles area) since 1974; also the year that they married. They are the proud parents of two adult sons; Ryan and Jonathan. Ed is a NAUI registered master scuba diver and enjoys snow skiing with his avid snowboarding sons.

Rigsbee Enterprises, Inc. — www.rigsbee.com
Cigar PEG-Philanthropy through Fun — www.cigarpeg.com